Functional Lessons in Singing

Functional Lessons in Singing

Second Edition

IVAN TRUSLER

Bowling Green State University
Bowling Green, Ohio

WALTER EHRET

Scarsdale High School
Scarsdale, New York

PRENTICE-HALL, INC., Englewood Cliffs, New Jersey

Printed in the United States of America

ISBN: 0–13–331801–x

Library of Congress Catalog Card No.: 73–180598

10 9 8 7 6 5 4 3 2 1

PRENTICE-HALL INTERNATIONAL, INC., London
PRENTICE-HALL OF AUSTRALIA, PTY. LTD., Sydney
PRENTICE-HALL OF CANADA, LTD., Toronto
PRENTICE-HALL OF INDIA PRIVATE LIMITED, New Delhi
PRENTICE-HALL OF JAPAN, INC., Tokyo

Contents

Preface

Purpose and Content

The purpose of this book is to present a functional series of lessons through which students may develop specific vocal and musical abilities with the sounds of the English language. The singer must work with vowels, diphthongs, and consonants. His skill is dependent upon how well he can apply these sounds in song.

After the first lesson, which seeks to establish proper breathing and breath control, each chapter takes up a different vowel, diphthong, or consonant. Words are read aloud, then sung. Sentences are sung. A study section follows which includes a description of the vowel, diphthong, or consonant and its proper execution. Common faults and how to correct them are included. General principles of singing are discussed in the first twelve lessons, and in each lesson there is an art song with a training text constructed on the sound being studied. Original texts are also included.

Special Features

All material is directly related to specific problems and goals. For example, a "Song interpretation and musicianship" section precedes *and is based upon* the art song in each lesson. Musical terms and interpretive and stylistic principles are learned *as they appear in each song*.

There are eighteen lessons, which fit the normal eighteen-week semester or thirty-six-week school year. All vowels, diphthongs, and consonants that a singer should use are included, with Webster and International Phonetic Alphabet symbols.

In addition to the song included with each lesson, there are eighteen more songs at the back of the book, making thirty-six in all, some of which were composed specifically for this book. A special feature, in Chapter 18, is the introduction of a song composed with twelve-tone row technique.

There is a selected, graded, and categorized list of song titles at the end of the book. A key to publishers is included.

Suggested Uses

This book is designed for use in the high school, college, conservatory, or church. It is a "class voice" book but is equally effective in the private studio. It is ideal as a training manual for mixed, treble, or male choirs and will also serve libraries as a reference text. The authors have based this book on many years of experience as musicians and educators. It works!

Ivan Trusler
Walter Ehret

1

Breathing and Breath Control

BREATHING EXERCISES

Good posture is the foundation of controlled breathing, and controlled breathing is the foundation of singing.

1. From a sitting position, lean forward, place forearms on the knees. Take a slow, deep, noiseless breath through the mouth. Expand the waistline entirely around the body, but do not raise the shoulders. The muscles in action are the abdominal (stomach), dorsal (back), and costal (rib). (See Figure 1–8)
2. Sit up with back straight and chest high. Repeat the breathing exercise 1 in this position.
3. Inhale deeply; then exhale slowly with a steady hissing sound for 24 counts. Continue to use abdominal, dorsal, and costal muscles.
4. Stand up with back straight, chest high, feet apart, with one foot slightly in front of the other. The weight is on the forward foot. Place hands on hips:

    Exhale: contract (pull in) the abdominal, dorsal, and costal muscles.

    Inhale deeply: allow the abdominal, dorsal, and costal muscles to expand. You should have a feeling of "lift" from the abdomen upward. Do not raise the shoulders.

    Exhale very slowly with a hissing sound as in exercise 3.

BREATH CONTROL EXERCISES

Hum these exercises on *M*. Continue breathing as instructed.

1. Very slowly.*

M   M   M   M   M   M   M   M

* The starting pitch of each exercise is comfortable for most voices but may be varied at the discretion of the teacher. This and all other exercises are to be repeated, transposing up and down by half-steps, throughout the entire vocal range.

2. Very slowly.

M M M M M

3. Slowly; be sure the second pitch (major third) is high enough.

M

4. Very slowly; sing with one breath.

M

5. Moderately; sing with one breath.

M

6. Very slowly.*

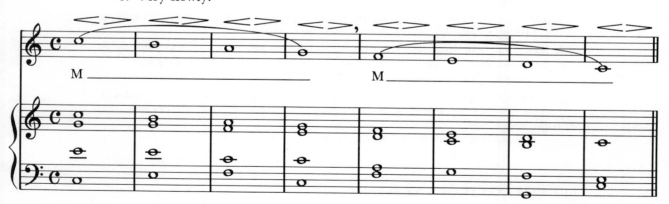

M M

7. Moderately; sing with one breath.

M

 * This descending scale is harmonized here for use throughout the book. Piano part can be used as a four-part choral experience.

STUDY

Correct breathing and breath control are largely dependent upon the action of the diaphragm and the rib cage. The diaphragm is a muscle wall situated between the stomach and the lungs. At rest, the diaphragm forms two semi-circular domes upon which the bases of the lungs rest. (See Figure 1-9.) During respiration (breathing), the diaphragm acts as follows:

1. *Inhalation* (Figure 1–2). The centers of the domes flatten, creating a space between the diaphragm and the lungs. Atmospheric pressure outside the body forces air through the respiratory tract into the decreased air pressure at the bottom of the lungs. The space fills with lung tissue.

2. *Exhalation*. The two domes return to their original positions, giving additional power to the expulsion of the breath. This action plays an important role in singing, providing energy and firm support at all dynamic levels throughout the range. The diaphragm is only partially responsible for respiration. As the rib cage is expanded, a larger cavity is formed which helps to force air into the lungs.

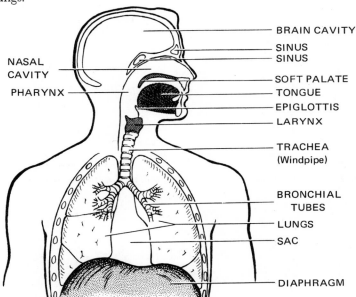

Figure 1-1

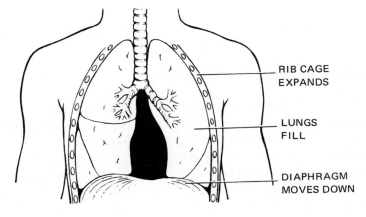

Figure 1-2

To feel the action of the diaphragm, place the tips of the fingers below the breast bone and cough. Note that before coughing, a deep inhalation takes place. Note the movement of the lower ribs and abdominal muscles.

Breathing: Common Faults and Corrections

Figures 1-3 and 1-4 show the two most common methods of breathing incorrectly; figures 1-5 and 1-6 show the correct method.

Poor posture is one of the chief causes of incorrect breathing. Good posture is essential to controlled breathing.

General Rules for Good Posture:
1. **Hold head comfortably erect.**
2. **Shoulders should remain down.**
3. **Carry chest high.**
4. **Keep back straight.**

Figure 1-3
High Chest Breathing (Incorrect)

Figure 1-4
Lower Abdominal Breathing (Incorrect)

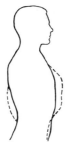

Figure 1-5
Diaphragmatic Breathing (Correct)

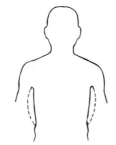

Figure 1-6
Costal Breathing (Correct)

Application of Breathing Principles to Singing

Deep, full breathing is prerequisite to a beautiful singing tone, and control of the breath is a vital part of such tone. Enrico Caruso, the great Italian tenor, said that he spent his entire life working for a maximum of tone while using a minimum of breath. Control of breath is usually dependent upon three factors:

The *diaphragm* controls the flow of air into and out of the lungs through the trachea (windpipe). Even though it has little muscle feeling, the diaphragm is under perfect mental control, responding to the singer's slightest wish as it works in a balanced action with the costal and abdominal muscles. The breathing system is both voluntary and involuntary: we can control breathing, and our bodies involuntarily breathe for us when we do not exercise conscious control.

The *vocal bands* (cords) resist the outgoing stream of breath from the trachea. Air passing through the vocal bands causes them to vibrate and produce tone. Figure 1-7 shows the vibration patterns of the vocal bands.

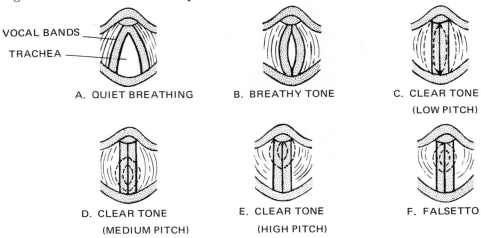

VOCAL BANDS

TRACHEA

A. QUIET BREATHING   B. BREATHY TONE   C. CLEAR TONE
(LOW PITCH)

D. CLEAR TONE   E. CLEAR TONE   F. FALSETTO
(MEDIUM PITCH)   (HIGH PITCH)

Figure 1-7

Even breath distribution increases and decreases in intensity as the song demands. If too much breath is expended, the vocal bands do not close properly, a breathy tone results, and control of the breath may be lost. Humming is an excellent device for developing clear tone production with a minimum of breath. Most beginning students produce good tone when the *M* hum is correctly sung; moreover, the *M* hum gives a feeling of free resonance.

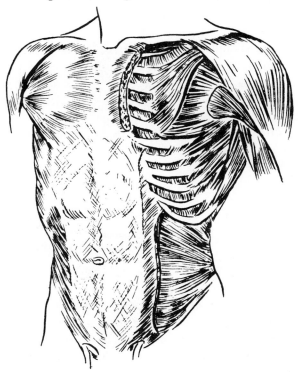

Figure 1-8 Stomach, Back, and Rib Muscles

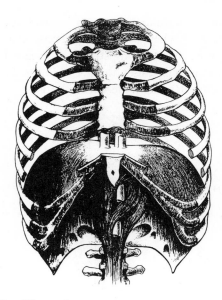

Figure 1-9
Diaphragm Muscle at Rest

General Rules for Humming:
1. **Lips should be loosely closed, tongue forward, throat relaxed.**
2. **Do not hum loudly, particularly in the upper range.**
3. **Do not hum below that part of the range in which the hum is clear.**
4. **Never hum louder than the volume necessary for a sense of free resonance.**

The clear hum is recognized by its purity of resonance and its feeling of freedom in production. Tone vibrations are most easily felt when one is humming in the lower ranges. To feel these vibrations, place the hand on the top of the head, nose, or back of the neck. The clear hum is so resonant that it seems to have an unrecognizable point of origin. Use humming for developing a clear tone and to examine resonance on every pitch of the range.

The singer must know not only how but also where to breathe. Examination of the text and music should reveal the correct places to take a breath. Do not depend on punctuation, especially commas. Find the musical phrases and breathe accordingly. For example, in the words, "Sleep my child, and peace attend thee, all through the night," do not breathe after *child*, for it makes more sense, musically speaking, to breathe after *thee* or *night*.

Markings are often inserted in printed music to indicate where to breathe. Those most commonly used are:

Apostrophe: ,

Rests: ━ ; ▬ ; ⸨ ; 𝄽 ; 𝄾

Curved lines which outline phrases:

General Rules for Breathing:
1. **In most songs, do not breathe between the syllables of a word.**
2. **Do not breathe between a noun and its modifier.**
3. **Do not break up a grammatical phrase or clause.**
4. **Do not destroy the rhythm of a song with inappropriate breaths.**
5. **Time for a breath should be taken from the final note of a phrase, not from the first note of a new phrase.**

SONG INTERPRETATION AND MUSICIANSHIP

All Through the Night, *Welsh Folk Song*

Hum and then sing in a *legato* (smooth, connected) style. The rhythm figure (♩. ♪) appears frequently. Do not sing this rhythm as a triplet ($\overset{3}{\sqcap}$), or as a double-dotted quarter note followed by a sixteenth note (♩.. ♪).

Music, like a building, is constructed according to a planned design. This design is called its "form." For example, in architecture when *split-level* or *ranch style* is used, these identify two different types, or styles, of houses. In music, *sonata* and *theme and variations* identify two large musical forms.

Songs may be *strophic,* in which the same music is repeated on different verses of the poem (as in hymns), or *through-composed,* which uses different music to follow the various changes in mood or meaning of each verse of the text, as in "The Erlking" by Schubert.

The most commonly used forms for songs are *two-part* and *three-part forms.* An example of a two-part song is "Greensleeves."

Part I
Alas! My love, you do me wrong,
To cast me off discourteously,
For I have loved you, oh, so long,
Delighting in your company.

Part II
Greensleeves was all my joy,
And, oh, Greensleeves was my delight,
Greensleeves, my heart of gold,
And all for Lady Greensleeves.

An example of a three-part song is "All Through the Night." Notice that measures 1-4, 5-8, and 13-16 are the same.* Measures 9-12 are different, and therefore contrasting. If we call measures 1-4, 5-8, and 13-16, the "A" sections, and 9-12 the "B" section (because it is different), we derive the following pattern:

A (A), B, A
or:
A (A) equals Part I
B equals Part II (requires contrasting treatment)
A (repeated) equals Part III

Thus we derive the name, "three-part form." Most folk songs, like "All Through the Night," are in simple forms. They should be sung with simplicity and sincerity. Spend most of your practice time humming this song. Words have been included as a guide for phrasing and mood, and for future use.

After each song throughout the book, a blank page of manuscript paper has been included for use by teacher and student.

* For easy reference, each measure of the song has been numbered.

ALL THROUGH THE NIGHT

James Boulton

Welsh Folk Song

Andante

1. Sleep my child, and peace at-tend thee, All Through The Night;
2. While the moon her watch is keep-ing, All Through The

Night; Guard - ian an - gels God will send thee,
Night; While the wea - ry world is sleep - ing,

All Through The Night; Soft the drow - sy
All Through The Night; O'er thy spir - it

hours are creep - ing, Hill and vale in slum - ber steep - ing,
gen - tly steal - ing, Vis - ions of de - light re - veal - ing,

I my lov - ing vi - gil keep - ing, All Through The Night.
Breathes a pure and ho - ly feel - ing, All Through The Night.

2

The *EE* Vowel

---

*Webster: ē

*International: i

WORDS WITH THE *EE* VOWEL

Read aloud slowly:

me	sleep	yield	weave
we	each	weep	leave
key	queen	see	keep
three	please	be	beat

Sing this exercise first on the *M* hum, to warm up. Start with the *M* hum on all exercises in subsequent lessons. Sing all words on the first note before moving on to the next.

1. Very slowly.

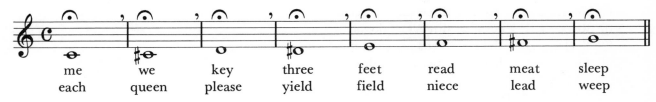

me	we	key	three	feet	read	meat	sleep
each	queen	please	yield	field	niece	lead	weep

2. Very slowly.

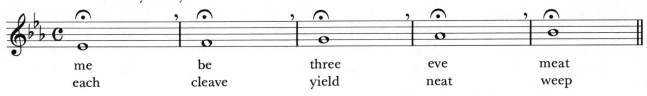

me	be	three	eve	meat
each	cleave	yield	neat	weep

* In this and all subsequent lessons, both Webster's diacritical symbols and the International Phonetic Alphabet symbols are given.

3. Very slowly; sing with one breath.

me _____	we _____	key
three _____	feet _____	read
meat _____	sleep _____	each
queen _____	please _____	yield

4. Moderately; sing with one breath.

me _____	we _____	key _____	three
feet _____	read _____	meat _____	sleep
each _____	queen _____	please _____	yield
field _____	niece _____	lead _____	weep

SENTENCES WITH THE *EE* VOWEL

Sing until *EE* vowels are clearly executed.

1. Very slowly.

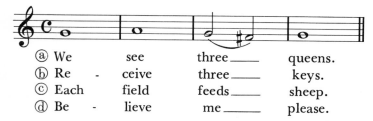

ⓐ We	see	three _____	queens.
ⓑ Re -	ceive	three _____	keys.
ⓒ Each	field	feeds _____	sheep.
ⓓ Be -	lieve	me _____	please.

2. Moderately; sing with one breath.

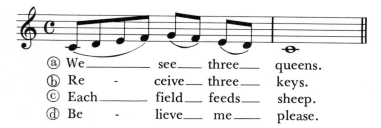

ⓐ We _____	see _____	three _____	queens.
ⓑ Re -	ceive _____	three _____	keys.
ⓒ Each _____	field _____	feeds _____	sheep.
ⓓ Be -	lieve _____	me _____	please.

3. Very slowly.

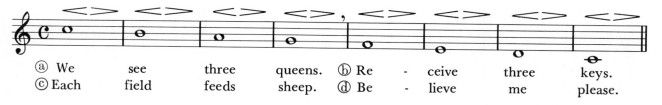

| ⓐ We | see | three | queens. | ⓑ Re - | ceive | three | keys. |
| ⓒ Each | field | feeds | sheep. | ⓓ Be - | lieve | me | please. |

4. Moderately; sing with one breath.

    ⓐ We_____   see   three___ queens._____
    ⓑ Re - ceive   three___ keys._____
    ⓒ Each_____ field   feeds___ sheep._____
    ⓓ Be - lieve   me___ please._____

STUDY

The *EE* (ē) Vowel:* Description and Execution

The *EE* vowel is a closed vowel. This means that the mouth is in a relatively closed position when singing *EE*. Resonate the *EE* vowel high and forward in the mouth. When singing *EE:*

1. The front of the tongue is raised in an arched position towards the roof of the mouth.
2. The tip of the tongue touches the rear of the lower front teeth.
3. The lips and teeth are parted slightly in a smiling position.
4. The lower jaw is relaxed.

Use a small hand mirror to check these positions as you practice.

The *EE* (i) Vowel: Common Faults and Corrections

Differentiate between *EE* and *IH* (it);† otherwise diction will not be clear and the meaning of the text will be impaired. If the *EE* vowel is not clear, *leave* becomes *live,* and *steal* becomes *still.* Form the *EE* vowel with the mouth relatively closed, resonating the vowel at the hard palate and through the nose. Do not allow the tone to sound pinched. Keep the jaw and lips free of tension. Think of the *EE* sound. Avoid a grinning smile which causes undue tension in the lips resulting in a lowered, too-relaxed palate and a nasal tone.

General Principles of Singing

Certain vowels are called primary or fundamental; others, secondary or subordinate. *EE* is a fundamental vowel.‡

The male voice must *cover* all vowels when singing full voice on high notes. To cover is to sing with a high degree of resonance concentrated at the hard palate and in the head and nasal cavities. The *EE* vowel lends itself readily to covering, since its normal position requires an intense palatal and head-cavity resonance.

---

  * Phonetic symbols used for "Description and Execution" are from the Webster system; the International Phonetic Alphabet is used for "Common Faults and Corrections."

  † The *IH* vowel is discussed in lesson 9.

  ‡ The next six lessons, excepting lesson 5, are devoted to fundamental vowels.

In the female voice, it is necessary to *open* all vowels when singing with full voice on high tones. Thus the *EE* vowel, although sung in a closed position in the middle and lower parts of the range, must be opened on the higher notes. The female singer should "think" the *EE* sound on high tones or clear diction will be obscured.

The word *resonance* has been used several times. There is good reason for this, for, after breathing, resonance is the most important consideration for the student of singing. Resonance determines the quality and color of the voice as well as its dynamic range. There are various kinds of resonance:

Induced resonance. A vibrating tuning fork held in the hand can be heard only if held close to the ear. If the shank of a vibrating fork is pressed against a table top, the tone can be heard throughout a large room. Thus the vibrations from the fork are transmitted to the table top which is forced to act as a sounding board. Many musical instruments function through induced vibration. For example, the vibrating strings on a violin are conveyed to the body of the instrument inducing resonance. This "sounding board" effect functions as we sing. Vibrations that can be felt in the chest when a low tone is sung are the result of induced vibrations conveyed from the larynx to the ribs and the sternum through the tissues of the neck and the bones of the spinal column.

Sympathetic resonance. Sit down at the piano and depress the "loud" pedal so that the strings are free to vibrate. Then sing various pitches up and down the scale. Soon you will sing a pitch that causes one of the piano strings to vibrate. The sound will be quite audible. You have sung the pitch to which that particular string is tuned, causing a "sympathetic" vibration.

Cavity resonance. Cavity resonators are tuned resonators; they will respond to only one pitch with maximum resonance. That response is determined by two factors: 1) the size of the cavity, 2) the size of the opening. The larger the cavity, the lower the pitch to which it responds; the larger the opening, the higher the pitch it will resonate. Thus a low pitch requires a large cavity with a small opening; a high pitch, a small cavity with a large opening.

Hold a vibrating tuning fork pitched at, for example, 440 cycles per second over the openings of a large variety of bottles. One bottle will greatly amplify the sound. If you then blow over the opening of that bottle, you will find that it has the same pitch (440 cycles) as the fork. Now take a large bottle with a small opening, hold the same vibrating fork at the opening, and gradually fill the bottle with water. Eventually, the tone will be greatly amplified. What you have done is reduce the volume of the bottle by adding water until its resonance cavity corresponds to the pitch of the fork—440 cycles. Another example of this form of resonance is the marimba. Its low notes require long tubes; its high notes have tubes that are small and short.

The vocal organs, from the larynx (voice box) upwards, can be likened to a kind of organ pipe which branches at the pharynx into two separate pipes, the mouth and the head (see Figure 2-1).

The mouth is the first resonator, producing the primary brilliance of the voice; the head with the nasal cavities is the second, providing the sonorous quality that is desirable. The chest is a third resonator, which produces vibrations below the larynx, providing depth and richness to the tone. We can change the shape of the mouth at will, and though we cannot change the shape of the nasal cavities and chest, we can control the extent to which we use them. All three are present in every tone, but we can control the proportion of one to the other for purposes of pitch, color, quality, and volume.

The different sounds that we sing are produced by changing the shape of the mouth and the position of the tongue and lips. For example, if we close the mouth, we may produce the sound studied in lesson 1, the *M* hum. By opening the mouth slightly, raising the front of the tongue, and spreading the lips, the *EE* vowel is produced.

As has been seen, pitch determines how sound is resonated. A low pitch seeks large resonance cavities (throat, chest, mouth); a high pitch seeks small resonance cavities (head, nasal cavities). Unlike most musical instruments, the voice has adjustable resonators; we can change the size and the opening of the mouth at will. We can therefore proportion resonance factors to suit pitch.

These facts explain why different tongue, lip, and jaw positions must be assumed for each of the sounds that we sing. This, together with the careful "tuning" of all the adjustable resonators of the voice is of supreme importance in singing, for the vocal bands send up a weak, simple, almost toneless pitch which is communicated to all the cavities it can reach and is resonated into vocal tone. *It is evenness of resonance throughout all pitches in the vocal range that must be mastered.*

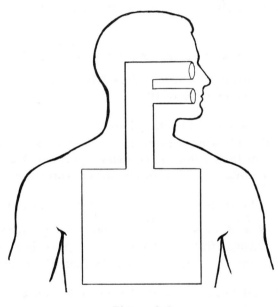

Figure 2-1

SONG INTERPRETATION AND MUSICIANSHIP

Largo, *Handel*

Memorize the following:

p (*piano*): soft

————— (*crescendo*): increasing power of tone

————— (*decrescendo*): decreasing power of tone

dolce: sweetly, softly, delicately

⁊ : take a breath

mf (*mezzo-forte*): medium loud

⌢ (*fermata*): pause or hold

allarg. (*allargando*): growing broader (i.e., louder and slower)

f (*forte*): loud

In the training text, every word is constructed on the *EE* vowel.*

Measures 1-15: These measures are known as the introduction. Attack the first note of the voice part as well as all others on pitch. Do not attack *below* the pitch and slide up.

Sing lyrically and smoothly, not vigorously or in a punched style.

General Rule:† Do not waste breath on the first notes of a phrase. Plan phrases to distribute breath evenly.

Measures 16-17: The following signs appear: $\longleftarrow$ $\longrightarrow$

This combination of crescendo and decrescendo over a single note or group of notes is known as a *messa di voce*. Practice this technique on single notes, then on longer phrases and vocalises (see exercise 17, this lesson) in order to develop finer control of the breath and voice. Mastery of *messa di voce* is indispensable for superior performance.

General Rule: Rarely is a long note or phrase sung without some dynamic variation. Seek to apply $<$ and/or $>$, or $<$ $>$ to long notes or phrases.

Measure 17: Execute *neath as* ♩. ♪ , not as ♩ ♩ or ♩ 𝄽 ♪ .

Measure 18: The word *trees* on ♩. should be sustained for three full beats and released on beat one of measure 19.

General Rule: Give all notes full value. Thus a ♩ note in 2/4 time is released on beat one of the following measure; a ♩. note in 4/4 time is released on beat four; a 𝅝 note in 4/4 time is released on beat one. Exceptions will occasionally occur for purposes of breathing and interpretation.

Measure 21: The word *these* must be executed on an even triplet ♩ ♩ ♩ ,

not as ♩ ♪ ♪ , ♪ ♪ ♩ or ♪ ♪. ♪ . Do not "scoop" these three notes. If necessary, practice them at first with an aspirate *h* (thee–hee–heez) to eliminate sliding and to define the pitch centers. Then eliminate the *h* and merely think it.

General Rule: Do not form the habit of using *h* for purposes of articulation. Clean articulation is brought about through coordinate action of the diaphragm against the breath. Continued use of the aspirate *h*, which causes a glottal stroke, may eventually damage the voice.

Measure 22: Take a breath at the end of the measure.

Measure 24: On the syllable *ceives,* do not slide down from the *E*-flat to the *B*-flat. Maintain a similar feeling of head resonance for the lower note as for the upper note.

General Rule: When notes abruptly drop from high to low, sing the lower note with a sensation of high resonance as on the upper note.

Measure 24: Execute the second *B*-flat (*me*) on exactly the same pitch as the first.

---

* Original texts are included for use in the future.

† *General rules*, which are important fundamental principles, will be mentioned only *once* throughout the volume. Observe these principles in all subsequent songs.

General Rule: Do not sing repeated notes flat. Imagine a repeated note to be higher than the note it follows.

Measure 26: Release *me* on the second half of beat 2 so that the next phrase may start on beat 3.

General Rule: New phrases must always start on the proper beat. Time for breathing is taken from the note preceding the new phrase. This is called a "catch" breath.

Measure 27: Stress slightly the tied-over *E*-flat on the first beat in order to bring out the syncopation (displacement of normal accent). Note that this type of tie occurs in measures 17, 34, and 37.

Measure 43: Slow down the tempo before going into the *fermata* (⌒).

General Rule: Fermatas are usually approached with a ritardando.

Measure 45: Observe the *allargando*.

Measures 47-52: These measures are the postlude.

This song, by the composer of the oratorio Messiah, *is from the first act of the opera* Xerxes.

LARGO

Ombra Mai Fu

George F. Handel
(1685—1759)

17

trees. Be - neath these sleep - y trees sweet peace re -
fu di ve - ge - ta - bi - le, ca - ra ed a -

ceives_____ me, re - ceives me. Sweet_____ peace re -
ma - bi - le, so - a - ve piu, ca - ra ed a -

ceives__me be - neath these__ trees. Be - neath these
ma - bi -le; Om - bra mai__ fu di ve - ge -

Sleep - y trees sweet peace re - ceives me, re - ceives
ta - bi - le, ca - ra ed a - ma - bi - le, so - a - ve

me, re - ceives me.
più, so - a - ve più.

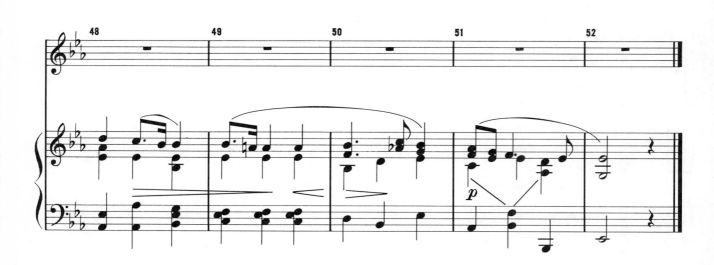

3

The *AY* Vowel

Webster: ā
International: eɪ

WORDS WITH THE *AY* VOWEL

Read aloud slowly:

may	stray	gray	pay
bathe	cake	hate	say
lathe	sane	straight	ray
lay	vein	jade	way

Sing.

1. Very slowly.

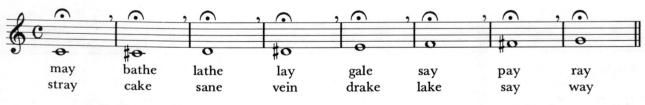

2. Very slowly.

3. Very slowly; sing with one breath.

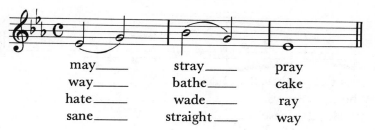

may____	stray____	pray
way____	bathe____	cake
hate____	wade____	ray
sane____	straight____	way

4. Moderately; sing with one breath.

gale____	drake____	knave____	claim
say____	lake____	paid____	came
bake____	fade____	rate____	day
pay____	say____	ray____	way

SENTENCES WITH THE *AY* VOWEL

Sing until all *AY* vowels are clearly executed.

1. Very slowly; sing with one breath.

ⓐ These	days	fade	a - way.
ⓑ Knaves	tease	sweet____	maids.
ⓒ Be	neat;	bathe each	day.
ⓓ Jake	hates	sweet____	cake.

2. Very slowly.

| ⓐ He | claims | we | paid. | ⓑ We | say | he | pays. |
| ⓒ May | we | speak | please? | ⓓ We | hail | thee | May! |

3. Moderately; sing with one breath.

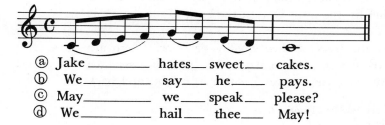

ⓐ Jake____	hates__ sweet__	cakes.
ⓑ We____	say__ he__	pays.
ⓒ May____	we__ speak__	please?
ⓓ We____	hail__ thee__	May!

4. Moderately; sing with one breath.

    ⓐ Jake_____ hates sweet___ cakes._____
    ⓑ We_____ say he___ pays. _____
    ⓒ May_____ we speak___ please?_____
    ⓓ We _____ hail thee___ May! _____

STUDY

The *AY* (ā) Vowel: Description and Execution

The *AY* vowel is an open vowel. The mouth should be more open when singing *AY* than when singing *EE*. The *AY* vowel always functions as the first part of a diphthong,* and is sung as follows:

1. The tip of the tongue touches the back of the lower front teeth.
2. The front of the tongue is lower than for *EE*.
3. The jaw is dropped slightly. The upper front teeth show in a smiling position wider than for *EE*. Allow the upper lip to rise slightly.

The *AY* (eɪ) Vowel: Common Faults and Corrections

Singers often substitute *EH* (men)† for *AY*. *AY* is a long vowel sound; *EH* is short. Note the difference in the following words:

AY (eɪ)	*EH* (ɛ)
may	met
bathe	bet
lathe	let
gay	get

Substituting *EH* for *AY* results in some frightful blunders. Thus: "*nail* on the roof" becomes "*Nell* on the roof" and "*wade* in the water" becomes "*wed* in the water." To avoid this, allow the lips to spread wider apart for *AY* than for *EH*, and keep the tongue in a higher arch.

General Principles of Singing

Vowels are classified as open or closed, depending on the relative size of the mouth opening. In addition, phoneticians (specialists in speech) classify sounds as either front or back, according to the position of the tongue. The front of the tongue (not the tip) is higher for the front vowels; the back of the tongue is higher for the back vowels.

Vowels are also classified on the basis of their quality or color. There are bright vowels and there are dark vowels, determined by the type of resonance characteristic of each vowel. All front vowels are classified as bright, and back

---

* For a discussion of diphthongs, see lessons 11 and 12.

† The *EH* vowel is discussed in lesson 9.

ones are classified as dark. *AY* and *EE,* because the front of the tongue is raised when they are sung, and because of the high proportion of palatal and head cavity resonance in each, are called "front, bright vowels."

Open vowels tend to be resonated farther back in the mouth and throat than are the closed vowels. All open and closed vowels must have palatal and head resonance. This is necessary for projection, production of tone which has carrying power.

One of the most important things for the student to know is that each vowel sound has its own individual quality. Nothing is so dull as a voice which has neutralized all vowels into one consistently bright or dark color. All qualities of the various vowel sounds should be used. As the student becomes proficient, he learns to color each vowel according to the meaning of the text. For example, joy or happiness might require a bright vowel color, death or lamentation a darker one. Listen to recordings of fine singers and notice how they color the vowels in order to enhance interpretation.

Classification of voices. Voices are divided into four general classes: soprano, alto, tenor, and bass. Various subdivisions, denoting the quality or style of the voice, occur within these classifications:

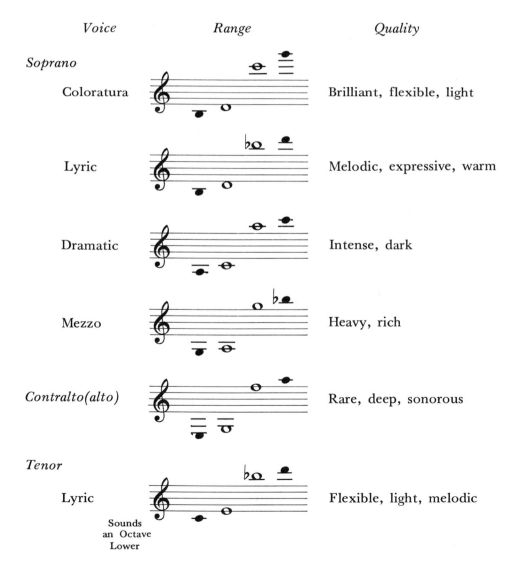

Voice	Range	Quality
Soprano		
Coloratura		Brilliant, flexible, light
Lyric		Melodic, expressive, warm
Dramatic		Intense, dark
Mezzo		Heavy, rich
Contralto(alto)		Rare, deep, sonorous
Tenor		
Lyric		Flexible, light, melodic

Sounds an Octave Lower

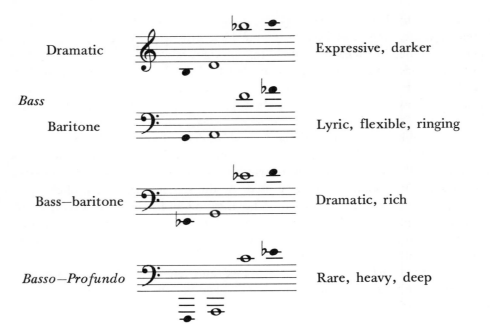

Dramatic		Expressive, darker
Bass		
Baritone		Lyric, flexible, ringing
Bass—baritone		Dramatic, rich
Basso—Profundo		Rare, heavy, deep

All classifications depend on quality and *tessitura* (general pitch position) as well as range. It sometimes takes several years of voice study before the voice can be classified. Meanwhile, the beginning student need worry only about using his voice properly so that vocal development will not be impeded.

SONG INTERPRETATION AND MUSICIANSHIP

Ave Maria, *Schubert*

The style of this song is *legato,* and it should be sung with reverence and deep religious feeling. Do not overemotionalize or sentimentalize.

Memorize the following:

pp (*pianissimo*): very softly

$>$ (*rinforzando*): accented

dim. (*diminuendo*): gradually diminishing the power of tone

ᴡ (*mordent*): a group of two or more grace notes played or sung rapidly before a principal note; consists of the principal note itself and the note above it. If notated, the *mordent* in measure 11 would appear as follows:

maid - en's

If the same sign is used with a vertical line through it, ᴡ , the lower auxiliary note is sung:

maid - en's

The training text of this song is made up almost entirely of words constructed on the *EE* and *AY* vowels.

Measures 1 and 2: The piano has a harp-like pattern. These notes should be played so that the rise and fall of the chordal pattern is gently curved. The left-hand octaves should not be thumped.

Measure 4: Sing the grace notes with delicacy. Practice these notes as a separate exercise until you are able to sing them with agility.

Measures 6 and 7: Do not slur the triplets so that there is a loss of pitch definition. Strive for clear, sharply defined movement between these notes, but do not lose the *legato* style. Do not sing with the aspirate in order to achieve clarity. Practice these triplets as a separate exercise.

Measure 7: Take a "catch breath" after *thee.*

Measure 8: Practice the grace note figure as an exercise for clarity and flexibility.

General Rule: When learning a melody to which grace notes have been added, practice the main melody notes without ornamentation. When these notes are secure, add the grace notes without disturbing the rhythmic flow. Do not sing the grace notes too rapidly. Give them time to "sound." The grace note is usually sung slightly before the beat in music composed after 1800.

Measure 11: The *mordent* appears. Practice it as a separate exercise until you can sing it smoothly.

Measure 11: The note is called an *appoggiatura. Appoggiatura* is taken from the Italian word *appoggiare* meaning "to lean against." It is one of the most charming embellishments of song and almost always has a yearning, sorrowful, or tender character. The cause of writing so long and accented a grace note lies in the fact that the *appoggiatura* is almost always extraneous to the melody and harmony with which it appears. Before an "even" note, the *appoggiatura* generally receives its face value—*i.e.,* one-half the value of the note which follows. Before a dotted note, it receives more than its face value—*i.e.,* two-thirds the value of the following note. In performance, the *appoggiatura* always receives the accent. If there is a diagonal line through this type of note

, it is sung twice as rapidly and is called an *acciaccatura,* a short

appoggiatura. Acciaccatura means "to crush."

Appoggiaturas in this song and in most music before 1800 should be sung *on* the beat.

Measure 12: The *appoggiatura* appears again.

Although students are urged to sing the training text, later on the Latin text should be learned and sung. Liturgical (church) Latin employs basically only five vowel sounds, which are easy to learn: *AH, EH, EE, AW, $\overline{OO}$.* Here is the text for Schubert's *Ave Maria* spelled phonetically. Stressed syllables are in capital letters.

Verse I

AH-veh Mah-REE-ah, GRAH-tsee-ah PLEH-nah
DAW-mee-noos TEH-koom,
Beh-neh-DEEK-tah TOO een Moo-lee-EH-ree-boos
eht beh-neh-DEEK-toos FROOK-toos VEHN-trees TOO-ee JEH-soos.

Verse II

AH-veh Mah-REE-ah, MAH-tehr DEH-ee
AW-rah praw NAW-bees peh-cah-TAW-ree-boos
NOONK eht een AW-rah MAWR-tees NAW-streh

AVE MARIA

Mary, We Hail Thee

Sir Walter Scott

Franz Schubert
(1797–1828)

1. Training text: Ma - ry we hail _____

2. Latin text:* 1. A - ve Ma - ri -

2. A - ve Ma - ri -

When singing in Latin, sing verses 1 and 2 and repeat verse 1 as a third verse.

29

maid.
na,
bis,

We - hail thee, hail thee as we
A - ve, A - ve! Do - mi -
O - ra, o - ra pro no -

pray, hail thee as we pray. Safe
nus, Do - mi - nus te - cum, Be - ne -
bis pec - ca - to - ri - bus, nunc

mp

may we keep be - neath thy care, 'though
di - cta tu in mu - li - e - ri - bus, et
et in ho - ra mor - tis, in

mp

30

32

4

The *AH* Vowel

Webster: ä
International: *a*

WORDS WITH THE *AH* VOWEL

Read aloud slowly:

Ma	farm	heart	far
ark	charm	mar	calm
barb	harm	march	dark
bar	dart	jar	psalm

Sing.

1. Very slowly.

ma	ark	barb	bar	car	dark	far	farm
charm	harm	dart	calm	garb	guard	heart	mar

2. Very slowly.

ma	charm	march	arch	heart
ark	harm	jar	palm	mar

3. Very slowly; sing with one breath.

large_____	mart_____	mark
Marge_____	smart_____	marsh
ma_____	car_____	dark
calm_____	garb_____	farm

4. Moderately; sing with one breath.

ma_____	ark_____	barb_____	ma
car_____	dark_____	far_____	car
charm_____	harm_____	dart_____	charm
garb_____	guard_____	heart_____	garb

SENTENCES WITH THE *AH* VOWEL

Sing until all *AH* vowels are clearly produced.

1. Very slowly.

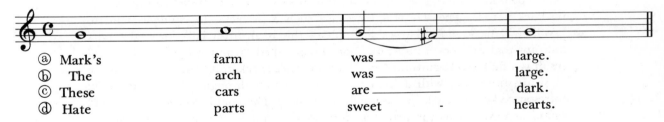

ⓐ Mark's	farm	was_____	large.
ⓑ The	arch	was_____	large.
ⓒ These	cars	are_____	dark.
ⓓ Hate	parts	sweet -	hearts.

2. Very slowly.

| ⓐ Weak | hearts | seek | calm. | ⓑ Dark | yards | need | light. |
| ⓒ These | days | are | calm. | ⓓ We | see | Dave's | arm. |

3. Moderately; sing with one breath.

ⓐ Mark's_____	farm - was_____	large.
ⓑ The_____	arch _ was_____	large.
ⓒ These_____	cars _ are _____	dark.
ⓓ Hate_____	parts sweet -	hearts.

4. Moderately; sing with one breath.

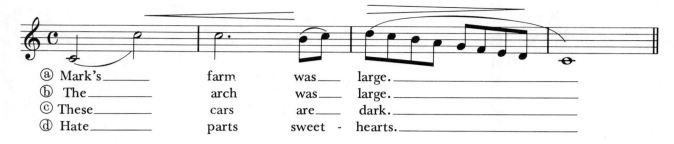

ⓐ Mark's_____ farm was___ large._____
ⓑ The_____ arch was___ large._____
ⓒ These_____ cars are___ dark._____
ⓓ Hate_____ parts sweet - hearts._____

STUDY

The *AH* (ä) Vowel: Description and Execution

The *AH* vowel is the most open of all vowels. It is the lowest of all the back vowels. *AH* is sung when Webster indicates *ä*. Fundamental *AH* is often followed by the consonant *r* and is executed as follows:

1. The tip of the tongue is forward, touching the back of the lower front teeth. The tongue lies relatively flat.
2. The jaw is dropped, but relaxed.
3. The lips are rounded easily forward.

The *AH* (*a*) Vowel: Common Faults and Corrections

As noted in lesson 3, it is difficult for students to achieve enough head resonance on back vowels. The *AH* vowel presents such a problem, for students tend to "swallow" the sound. The visible result of this is an artificially lowered larynx and lips that are too protuberant (sometimes called "trumpet lips"). The aural result is a dull, thick, guttural tone. To avoid this, speak and then sing a sequence of words beginning with a front vowel, proceeding through others which tend to resonate farther back in the mouth and chest. The goal is to keep the second sound as resonant as the first, the third as resonant as the second, and so on. Thus:

EE(i) ⌣ AY(eɪ) ⌣ AH(*a*)
We ⌣ stay ⌣ smart
She ⌣ plays ⌣ cards

Apply this principle to the exercises at the beginning of the lesson. Note that fundamental *AH* is represented by the spelling *a* in all words studied in this lesson. There are other words, however, which require fundamental *AH* that are spelled with *o*. Some of these are *odd, hot, box, cop, God, lot, rot,* and *pot*. Do not substitute the vowel *AW* (lesson 6) or medial *AH* (lesson 5). Use fundamental *AH*.

General Principles of Singing

As the student begins to sing solos in public, if only in front of the voice class, he should become concerned with stage deportment. Effectiveness as a singer depends not only upon the voice and choice of songs, but also upon a good platform manner.

36

When singing, one should be poised, with an air of dignity and sincerity. If one appears ill at ease, the audience will respond in kind. Modest assurance is the ideal manner, and nothing begets assurance like intelligent practice and vocal skill. There are certain standard procedures of stage etiquette which should be observed:

1. A woman always precedes a man on and off the stage, regardless of which is the accompanist or soloist. When both accompanist and soloist are of the same sex, the soloist enters and leaves first.
2. The soloist's entrance is made with a quick but graceful walk to a definite spot, usually the "crook" of the piano. He does not run or lag.
3. When he reaches the desired spot, if he has been greeted by applause, he acknowledges the courtesy with a graceful bow. He places one foot behind the other, shifts his weight to the rear foot, and bends forward slightly from the waist. The bow fits the personality and physique.
4. What to do with the hands is a problem for many singers. The custom is to hold the hands together at the waistline. It is wise not to raise and extend them while singing, for this gives an unnatural and affected appearance. Posing and affectation are for singers who do not have talent enough to do without them.
5. When the audience is quiet and ready to listen, a slight nod is given to the accompanist as a signal to begin.
6. If there is an introduction, and if there are interludes, the soloist maintains an attentive attitude.
7. The mood of the song is reflected in the general manner of singing. One voice teacher has said that the singer should "look like the music."
8. When singing, the soloist looks above the heads of the audience and does not stare fixedly at one spot. He avoids glancing about in a nervous, restless manner.
9. When he has a solo with a chorus, he must remember that the one unforgivable sin in performance is to make a mistake because he has not been watching the conductor.
10. At the end of a song, he should not bow before the applause begins.
11. An encore is not sung unless the applause calls for one.

The best way to learn good stage deportment is to watch the stage presence of seasoned professional singers.

SONG INTERPRETATION AND MUSICIANSHIP
Caro Mio Ben, *Giordani*

The tempo mark, *andante con moto,* means "flowing easily" (*andante*), "with motion" (*con moto*).
Memorize the following:

rit. (*ritardando*): delaying the time gradually

più: more

poco: little

accel. (*accelerando*): gradually increasing the speed of the movement

e: and

port. (*portamento*): from *portare* meaning "to carry." Indicates a carrying or gliding of the tone from one note to the next, but so rapidly that the intermediate notes are not defined

a tempo: in time; a term used to denote that after some deviation or relaxation of the tempo, the performer must return to the regular tempo

The training text of this song has been made up almost entirely of words constructed on the *EE, AY,* and *AH* vowels.

Measure 3: The figure ♪. ♪ must not be executed as ♩ ♪. Feel the ♪ as belonging to the following ♩ rather than to the combination ♪. ♪.

Measure 6: Grace notes (short *appoggiaturas*) appear. Practice this entire measure daily to develop flexibility.

Measure 13: Increase speed: prepare to slow down on the last two beats of measure 14.

Measures 13-19 have considerable variation in both tempo and dynamics. Rehearse the following separately:

1. Practice the tempo changes only (*poco accel., piu allargando, a tempo*). At first, exaggerate these shifts of speed. This should make you more conscious of the changes. When fully aware of them, work toward more subtle contrasts in speed.
2. Practice the dynamic changes (◁ ▷) in steady tempo. At first, exaggerate these changes. Then, when aware of the various dynamic levels, work toward a more musical variation within the framework of correct tempos.

Measure 19: Note the *portamento.* Make the glide from pitch *A* to pitch *D* in measure 20 without giving definition to the intermediate pitches. *Do not* take a breath between these notes.

Although students are urged to continue step-by-step through this book, exploring the characteristics of one sound at a time, some may wish at this point to extend their musical and vocal experiences beyond the songs and training texts in each lesson. To this purpose eighteen additional songs are included at the end of the book. One of these, Igor Stravinsky's *Pastorale,* page 185, employs the *AH* vowel almost exclusively. This lovely and early song of the great composer should be sung quite slowly and softly, never getting louder than *mf.* For basses and altos, the key of F-sharp major may be too high, in which case transpose down to the key of E major.

In the eighteenth century, interpolations were a customary practice among singers. Passages so inserted called for a high degree of technical skill from the performer and reflected his virtuosity. Although "Caro Mio Ben" is a relatively simple example of eighteenth-century song, it requires the embellished style. At the discretion of the teacher, this should include trills, appoggiaturas, and the general "filling up" of intervals at appropriate places.

CARO MIO BEN

Ah! My Dear Heart

Giuseppe Giordani
(1753–1798)

41

I grieve for thee.

lan - gui - sce il cor.

5

The Medial *AH* Vowel

Webster: ȧ, ă, ī
International: æ

WORDS WITH THE MEDIAL *AH* VOWEL

Read aloud slowly:

	Pure		*Diphthongs**
man	dance	last	I
can	mask	chance	my
ran	fast	can't	sigh
an	past	laugh	fine

Sing

1. Very slowly.

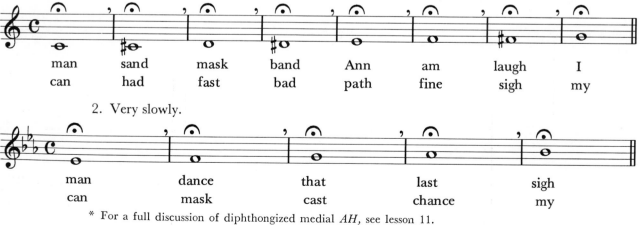

man	sand	mask	band	Ann	am	laugh	I
can	had	fast	bad	path	fine	sigh	my

2. Very slowly.

man	dance	that	last	sigh
can	mask	cast	chance	my

* For a full discussion of diphthongized medial *AH*, see lesson 11.

3. Very slowly; sing with one breath.

man_____	can_____	fine
an_____	sigh_____	had
and_____	dance_____	I
fast_____	my_____	ask

4. Moderately; sing with one breath.

Ann_____	can't_____	my_____	fine
past_____	path_____	laugh_____	sigh
sand_____	ask_____	mast_____	glass
prance_____	had_____	band_____	half

SENTENCES WITH THE MEDIAL *AH* VOWEL

Sing until all vowels are clearly produced.

1. Very slowly; sing with one breath.

ⓐ Can	that	man_____	laugh?
ⓑ Mike	and	Jane_____	sigh.
ⓒ We	like	that_____	band.
ⓓ An	aged	man_____	passed.

2. Very slowly.

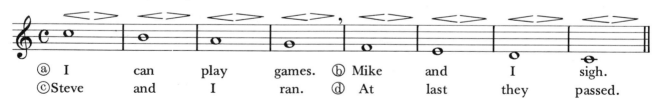

| ⓐ I | can | play | games. | ⓑ Mike | and | I | sigh. |
| ⓒ Steve | and | I | ran. | ⓓ At | last | they | passed. |

3. Moderately; sing with one breath.

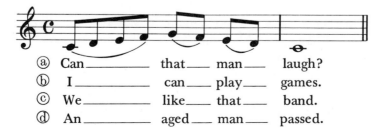

ⓐ Can_____	that_____	man_____	laugh?
ⓑ I_____	can_____	play_____	games.
ⓒ We_____	like_____	that_____	band.
ⓓ An_____	aged_____	man_____	passed.

4. Moderately; sing with one breath.

@ She_____ can play___ fine._____

ⓑ Mike_____ and Jane___ dance._____

ⓒ Steve_____ and I ___ sigh._____

ⓓ At_____ last thay___ passed._____

STUDY

The Medial *AH* (à, ă, ī) Vowel: Description and Execution

The medial *AH* vowel is an open, front vowel. It is the lowest of the front vowel sounds—that is, the tongue is lower than for any other front, bright vowel. The term *medial* is used to denote this vowel's place between the front, bright *AY* sound and the back, dark *AH* sound.

The medial *AH* does not appear in either the Italian or German tongues and is often overlooked by singers trained exclusively in European literature. It is always spelled with the letter *a* except in diphthongs and appears in stressed syllables more frequently than any other *a* in the English language.

When *ī* is given, medial *AH* is combined with *IH* to form a diphthong (*mine, vine, I*). The vowel is sung the same whether pure or the first part of a diphthong.

To sing medial *AH* correctly:

1. The tip of the tongue touches the lower front teeth.
2. The front of the tongue is only slightly arched and is lower than for *EE* and *AY*.
3. The jaw is dropped less than for the more open, fundamental *AH*.
4. The lips are in a smiling position.

Medial *AH* is used in singing when Webster gives either *à* or *ă*. There is a difference in shading between these vowels, but it is so slight that the adjustment is made without conscious effort. The student will notice, after careful examination, that the front of the tongue is slightly lower for *à* than for *ă*. Read, then sing, the following words:

à	ă
laugh	fat
aunt	man
ask	ran
fast	can

The Medial *AH* (æ) Vowel: Common Faults and Corrections

Do not substitute *AH* (farm) for medial *AH*. Except when singing extremely high tones, this procedure sounds affected and unnatural, and is unacceptable in good English. When this is done, *hand* becomes *hahnd*, *man* becomes *mahn*, and *can* becomes *cahn*. Your ear must help you avoid this mistake, although certain mechanical means will also help. Widen the sides of the tongue and the corners of the mouth when singing medial *AH*. Keep the soft palate high (check with a hand mirror), or a distressing nasal twang may result. This applies particularly to words like *France, dance,* and *prance.* It may be helpful to approach medial *AH* through *AH* (farm) by slowly speaking and then singing the following words in sequence:

AY (eɪ)	*AH* (a)	*medial AH* (æ)
mate	mart	mad
hate	heart	had
late	lard	lad
bait	bard	bad

Keep the soft palate as high for medial *AH* as for *AY* and *AH* (farm).

Do not substitute *EH* for medial *AH* in words which have the consonant *r* or "double *r*." Thus:

marry	becomes	*merry*
Paris	"	*Perris*
Carol	"	*Cerol*
paradise	"	*peradise*

Speak and sing these words until you can avoid this mistake.

General Principles of Singing

It was mentioned before that the ear must be trained to help the student avoid mistakes. *Hearing* plays just as important a part in singing as do *observation* and *technique*. One may *observe* a good singer, and one may build *technique,* but the end result is dependent upon one's ability to *hear* what beautiful tone and expression are.

We study singing to build a technique through which to express songs. Everyone agrees that expressiveness is paramount; technique by itself is almost worthless. But expression without technique is impossible. The singer must enlarge his powers of expression, his ability to project song, his understanding of style, phrasing, and nuance, while he builds his technique. These are principles of singing upon which all knowledgeable musicians agree.

SONG INTERPRETATION AND MUSICIANSHIP

Dedication, *Franz*

The *tempo* is marked *Andante espressivo* which means "flowing easily" (*andante*), "with expression" (*espressivo*). Memorize the following:

(in piano part) *arpeggio*: play the notes of a chord consecutively in harp style. The *arpeggio* begins on the beat and starts with the lowest note.

The training text of this song has been made up almost entirely of words constructed on the *EE, AY, AH,* and medial *AH* vowels.

All fine music has meaningful groups of notes that are related melodically, harmonically, and rhythmically. These groups of notes, often four to eight measures long, are called *phrases*. When learning songs, always think in terms of the phrase rather than of individual notes. Most phrases have a rise and fall of dynamics, as does the first phrase of this song. In addition, each phrase usually has a note or group of notes of climax. The approach to and away from these phrase climaxes must be carefully planned. Each phrase must also relate to other phrases, so that when combined in a song, they form a logical, artistic whole. To phrase properly, one should be conscious of:

Words. The relative importance of words in a sentence, as well as the mood they are projecting, must be understood. It is often helpful to recite the words alone, speaking them as an actor would. When understood, they should be sung with the same expression as when recited.

Melody. Melodic lines have a "curve" or "arch" which create a feeling of tension as the phrase climax is approached, and a feeling of relaxation as the climax is passed. Sensitivity to this give and take in the melodic line will make singing more intelligible and musical.

Harmony. The accompaniment is a vital aid to the singer's phrasing. Harmonies and pianistic patterns give hints as to dynamic and tempo variations, mood, and word stress.

Analyze "Dedication" with your teacher and other singers. Note that each phrase has been marked with a slur (⌒). Make specific plans so that each phrase is meaningful both as a unit and as a part of the song as a whole. Here are some questions to answer about each phrase:

1. What are the key words?
2. What are the "mood" or "color" words?
3. How wide is the dynamic range? Is the $<$ $>$ . . . in measure 2 the same as in measure 5 or measures 11–12?
4. Are there phrases that speed up or slow down?
5. Where is the *melodic* note (notes) of climax? Does the harmony in the accompaniment help to determine this?
6. Where is the *dynamic* climax?
7. How does phrase 1 relate to phrase 2? How do these relate to other phrases?
8. What is the climax of the selection? Has it been properly prepared by the growth of the phrases leading to it? If the climax is not at the end of the piece, how are the measures following the climax to be sung?

Although outstanding singers leave some of their artistry to the "inspiration of the moment," most great and true expression is the result of painstaking effort and thoughtful planning. Review the songs previously learned, utilizing these ideas.

On page 187 may be found another lovely and contrasting song with many medial *AH* vowels—"My Lovely Celia" by George Monro. This song in strophic form should be sung very simply but with expression. Practice the florid passages slowly at first, making sure the vowels are pure. Observe dynamic markings carefully. Do not make the mistake of taking the words too seriously. Approach them with tongue-in-cheek humor. George Monro was an eighteenth-century organist and composer. Many secular songs of this period were set to texts of unrequited love. "My Lovely Celia" is one of these.

Robert Franz is one of the most important representatives of the German Lied. His compositions and arrangements include 257 songs, all of which were composed originally for a single kind of voice, the medium voice. He did not write dramatic ballads; he excluded from his songs all that was passionate or extreme in feeling.

DEDICATION

Widmung

Wolfgang Muller

Andante espressivo

Robert Franz
(1815–1892)

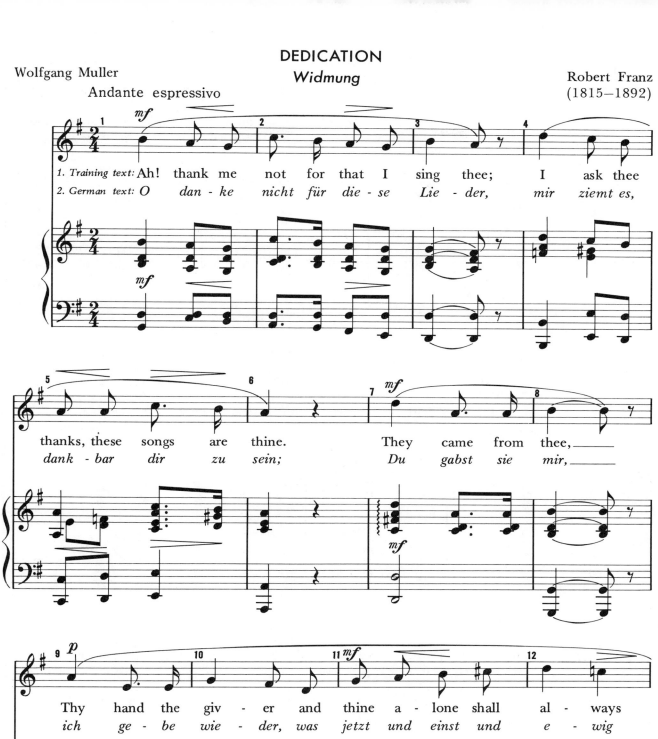

1. Training text: Ah! thank me not for that I sing thee; I ask thee
2. German text: O dan - ke nicht für die - se Lie - der, mir ziemt es,

thanks, these songs are thine. They came from thee,_____
dank - bar dir zu sein; Du gabst sie mir,_____

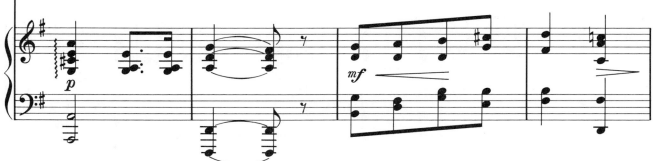

Thy hand the giv - er and thine a - lone shall al - ways
ich ge - be wie - der, was jetzt und einst und e - wig

49

be.

dein.

Thine are these songs, the gift and

Dein sind sie al - le ja ge -

giv - er, the light_____ from thy dear eyes to mine

we - sen, aus dei - ner lie - ben Au - gen Licht

gave an ex - am - ple, gave un - der - stand - ing.

hab' ich sie treu - lich ab - ge - le - sen,

Dost thou not know____ that these____ are thine?____
kennst du die eig - nen Lie - der nicht?____

Dost thou not know____ that these____ are thine?____
Kennst du die eig - nen Lie - der nicht?____

6

The aw Vowel

Webster: ô
International: ɔ

WORDS WITH THE *AW* VOWEL

Read aloud slowly:

all	drawl	jaw	mall
awe	fawn	law	yawn
ball	fall	lawn	pause
paw	Gaul	Maud	raw

Sing.

1. Very slowly.

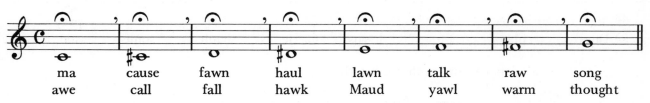

ma	cause	fawn	haul	lawn	talk	raw	song
awe	call	fall	hawk	Maud	yawl	warm	thought

2. Very slowly.

talk	yawl	yawn	pause	raw
song	thought	long	cause	gone

53

3. Very slowly; sing with one breath.

ma	call	gone
law	talk	awe
dawn	gauze	lawn
long	cause	yawn

4. Moderately; sing with one breath.

ma _____	cause _____	fawn _____	haul
lawn _____	talk _____	raw _____	awe
call _____	law _____	hawk _____	maul
dog _____	gone _____	long _____	song

SENTENCES WITH THE *AW* VOWEL

Sing until all vowels are clearly produced.

1. Very slowly.

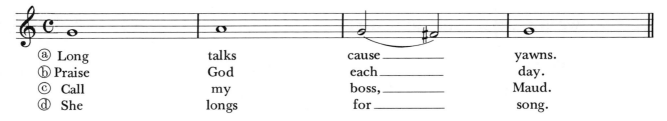

ⓐ Long	talks	cause _____	yawns.
ⓑ Praise	God	each _____	day.
ⓒ Call	my	boss, _____	Maud.
ⓓ She	longs	for _____	song.

2. Very slowly.

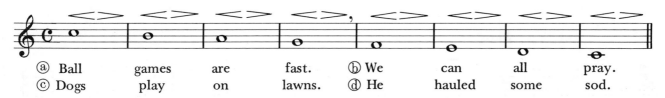

ⓐ Ball	games	are	fast.	ⓑ We	can	all	pray.
ⓒ Dogs	play	on	lawns.	ⓓ He	can	hauled	some	sod.

3. Moderately; sing with one breath.

ⓐ Long _____	talks __ cause __	yawns.
ⓑ Praise _____	God __ each __	day.
ⓒ Call _____	my __ boss, __	Maud.
ⓓ She _____	longs __ for __	song.

4. Moderately; sing with one breath.

ⓐ Ball_____	games	are___	fast._____
ⓑ We_____	can	all___	pray._____
ⓒ Dogs_____	play	on___	lawns._____
ⓓ He_____	hauled	some__	sod._____

STUDY

The *AW* (ô) Vowel: Description and Execution

The *AW* vowel is an open vowel. Like *AH* (*farm*), it is a back vowel, but much darker. *AW* is produced as follows:

1. The back of the tongue is raised in an arched position, slightly higher than for *AH* (*farm*).
2. The tip of the tongue is forward.
3. The lips are pursed, forming an oval shape. The corners of the mouth are drawn easily toward each other. The jaw is down.

The *AW* (ɔ) Vowel: Common Faults and Corrections

In some sections of the country, *AH* (*farm*) is mistakenly substituted in most words that should be pronounced *AW*. Singers should change this localized pronunciation to standard pronunciation. Words in which this substitution is most likely to occur are those which have in their spellings: *al, ald, alk, all, alt, au, aught,* and *aw.* Practice speaking and singing the following words, using *AW,* not *AH.*

also	bald	talk*	call	salt	cause	taught	law
always	scald	walk*	ball	exalt	fault	daughter	saw

General Principles of Singing

In all lessons up to this point, the *legato* style has been stressed: the linking together of words has been emphasized. There are phrases within which words should not be joined, however, even when one sings in the *legato* style. Three rules concern phrases in which words are separated:

1. When a word ends in the same vowel *sound* with which the next word begins, the words are separated. For example, sing:

the / east	not	*theeast*
the / eve	not	*theeve*

This rule applies only when the *sound* is the same. When the sounds are different, even when spelled with the same letter, the words are connected. This rule also applies to diphthongs. Thus: "say / it," not "sayit," because the *AY* vowel in *say* ends with *IH,* the same sound that begins *it.*

* The letter *l* in these words is silent.

2. When diction may be obscured, the words are separated. For example, in column I below, separate the words, or they will sound like the word in column II.

	I	II
	round / eyes	dies
	whose / eyes	sighs
	name / any	many
	hear our prayer / O Lord	row

Exceptions to this rule are determined by the relative importance of the words within a phrase. In "O Lord of Hosts," the word *Lord* is so important, and the word *of* so unimportant, that "Lord of" can be connected without fear of loss of meaning. On the other hand, in the phrase, "Let us pray," the important word is *pray*. If *us* is connected with *pray,* the invitation will seem to be, "Let us spray!"

3. When a word beginning with a vowel requires extra stress to heighten the dramatic effect, the words are separated. For example, sing:

O / endless / agony! (stress *e*ndless *a*gony)
He is / ill! (stress *i*ll)
Where / are you? (stress *a*re)

This rule applies only in situations which require dramatic effect.

SONG INTERPRETATION AND MUSICIANSHIP

Calm As the Night, *Bohm*

The tempo is marked *tranquillo,* which means to sing in a restful, quiet manner.

Memorize the following:

⌒······· (piano part): semi-*legato*

The training text has been constructed so that many *AW* vowels are included.

Throughout this volume, each song introduces or emphasizes a technical problem pertaining to either vowels or consonants. In studying these songs, it is helpful at first to sing the melodies with *neutral syllables* rather than the text that is provided. Neutral syllables are combinations of vowels and consonants which help to serve the purposes of vocalization (*mee, may, mah, maw*). They can be helpful in isolating a vowel or consonant problem and providing means to remedy that problem. For example, this song could be sung first on the neutral syllable *maw,* prior to the use of words, if the student is having difficulty singing *AW.* Apply neutral syllables to all songs throughout this volume.

Measure 11: Always return to the *original* tempo after singing the *ritardando.* Singers tend to return to a tempo *slower* than the original after they have sung a *ritardando.*

Measure 36: Do not sing *the* on the sixth beat of the measure. It occurs on the *second half* of the sixth beat. Think of this note as being connected to *Sun* rather than to *as.*

Measure 37: The same problem is encountered on the word *and.*

Measures 36-39: Do not strain or force the voice. This phrase has a high *tessitura* and is quite demanding. Sing no louder than you can sing with good tone. Observe the *con moto.*

Observe the breath marks throughout this song. Plan each phrase so that breath is distributed evenly. Breath marks are not included where rests appear.

As a supplementary song for this lesson, try the lovely Southern Mountain tune, "He's Gone Away" on page 190. Sing with great simplicity and freedom. Note that there are measures which are uneven in length ($\frac{4}{4}$ $\frac{3}{4}$ $\frac{4}{4}$ $\frac{2}{4}$). Keep the length of the quarter note the same in all these measures. The accompaniment has been arranged for piano, but someone may wish to accompany this song with guitar. Try it! If played well, guitar accompaniment is most effective.

This song was written by the German pianist and salon composer, Carl Bohm. It is his best-known composition and is a favorite among both professional and amateur singers.

CALM AS THE NIGHT
Still Wie die Nacht

Carl Bohm
(1844—1920)

1. Training text: Calm as the night, Strong as the Sea,
2. German text: *Still wie die Nacht, tief wie das Meer,*

57

7

The *OH* Vowel

Webster: ō
International: ou

WORDS WITH THE *OH* VOWEL

Read aloud slowly:

oh	dope	hope	load
boat	dole	hold	lore
bode	fold	hose	more
cove	foe	Joe	moan

Sing:

1. Very slowly.

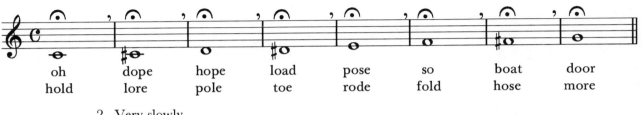

oh	dope	hope	load	pose	so	boat	door
hold	lore	hope	pole	toe	rode	fold	hose	more

2. Very slowly.

oh	hold	prone	cold	jolt
dope	lore	told	flow	knows

3. Very slowly; sing with one breath.

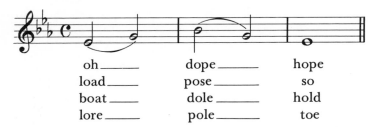

oh ____	dope ____	hope
load ____	pose ____	so
boat ____	dole ____	hold
lore ____	pole ____	toe

4. Moderately; sing with one breath.

oh ____	hold ____	prone ____	cold
jolt ____	dope ____	lore ____	told
flow ____	knows ____	hope ____	poke
cove ____	joke ____	rose ____	load

The vocalises to this point have been the same in each lesson. For variety, and to introduce students to minor keys, sentences in this and the next five lessons will be based on different vocalises. Number 1 below introduces c minor. Students will note that the key signature is the same as for E-flat major. Relative minor scales always begin a third below their major and have the same key signature. Here is a chart of all the major keys and their relative minor keys. Memorize the chart. Go back to each song studied so far and discover its key. Do this for all songs in the future.

Flat keys   Relative Minor Keys   Sharp keys   Relative Minor Keys

Note that in exercise 2, in the fourth and fifth measures, there is a b-natural. This is called a *harmonic* minor. When the seventh pitch in a minor scale is raised, the scale is called a harmonic minor scale. Note that in exercise 4, measure one, both pitch *a* and pitch *b* are natural. In the third measure, these two pitches are flatted again. This is called a *melodic* minor. When the sixth and seventh pitches are raised going up in a minor scale and are lowered going down, the scale is called a melodic minor scale. When all pitches remain the same going both up and down in a minor scale, the scale is called a *natural* minor scale.

SENTENCES WITH THE *OH* VOWEL

1. Very slowly.

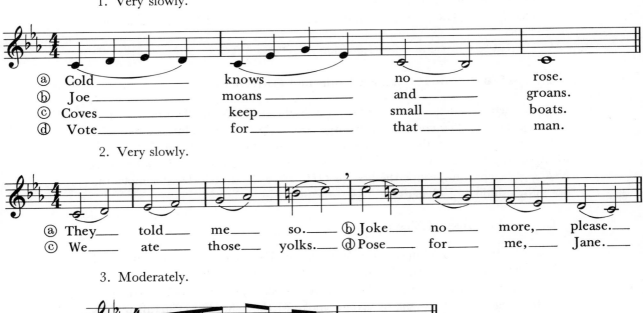

2. Very slowly.

3. Moderately.

4. Sing with one breath.

STUDY

The *OH* (ō) Vowel: Description and Execution

The *OH* vowel is an open vowel, although less open than *AW*. Like *AW*, *OH* is a back, dark vowel and should have a mellow, rich resonance. *OH* is a pure sound (Webster ō) *only* in words in which it is unstressed. For example, *OH* is pure in "*o*bey," "*o*vert," "p*o*lite," and "mem*o*ry." When *OH* is pure, it is spelled *o*. *OH* is diphthongized in all words and exclamations of one syllable (*oh, no, cold, rose*) and in all words of more than one syllable within which it receives any stress (*only, devotion, motion*). When diphthongized, *OH* is combined with *O͜O* (*look*).* *OH* is sung the same way, whether it is pure or the first part of a diphthong:

1. The back of the tongue is raised higher than for *AW*.
2. The tip of the tongue is forward.
3. The lips are allowed to purse farther forward than for *AW*, forming an oval shape.
4. The jaw is down in a relaxed position.

The *OH* (OU) Vowel: Common Faults and Corrections

Do not tense the lips, for this results in a "tight" tone. Allow the lips to round, but keep the rounding comparatively large. Do not protrude the lips too much.

In some sections of the United States, *OH* is attacked with an *EH* sound, followed by a "glide" into pure *OH*. Thus, *go* becomes *geh͡ o*, and *blow* becomes *bleh͡ o*. To avoid this, shape the lips for *OH* before the attack. Do not move the lips into position *after* the attack.

General Principles of Singing

Good health plays an important role in fine singing. When a singer is in "good voice," the condition can usually be attributed to a balanced diet, proper exercise, rest, and other essentials of good health. Singers, like athletes, should have their own training rules. They should avoid smoking; they should get a full night's rest each night in a well-ventilated room; they should establish a balanced diet including multi-vitamin supplements if necessary; and they should exercise out-of-doors each day if only by taking a long, brisk walk.

Observe the following rules of vocal hygiene:

Do not abuse your voice. Yelling and cheer-leading at athletic contests may be good school spirit, but they are deadly for the voice. Go to the games or play in them, but contribute your portion of cheer without yelling.

Make rest periods as important as practice periods. Like other parts of the body, the muscles of speech and the vocal organs require rest after usage. These muscles work almost twice as much when singing as when speaking. In speaking it is estimated that the vocal bands phonate about *45 per cent to 50 per cent* of the time; in singing, about *90 per cent to 95 per cent* of the time. Arrange your schedule so that there is ample rest between practice periods. Do not practice early in the morning or immediately after a heavy meal. Develop note-reading ability, so that you can learn songs by reading them over silently.

* For a discussion of diphthongized *OH*, see lesson 11.

Sing carefully when you have a head cold or minor throat irritation. These conditions are not injurious to the vocal bands when the tone is produced correctly. If, however, breathing begins to be affected, *stop singing.*

Never force the voice. Never sing louder than you can sing with a good tone. A forced tone is *always* a bad tone.

If laryngitis develops, see your physician and do not speak or sing for the duration of the infection.

Two common results of the misuse of the voice are:

Tremolo. A tremolo is an excessive waver in the voice which causes distortion of the desired pitch. Tremolos may be fast, resembling a goat bleat, or slow, characterized by an undulation or wobble. In both cases, they are undesirable and can be corrected only by rest and proper attention to posture, breathing, and elimination of excessive tension in the muscles of speech and the vocal organs. Tremolo should not be confused with *vibrato.* A warm, natural vibrato is essential for a lovely tone. Vibrato is a regular sequence of "beats" produced by the fully resonated voice and does not obscure the tonal center.

Vocal nodes. Vocal nodes are tiny, hardened spots, resembling callouses, which form on the margins of the vocal bands. Continued misuse of the voice causes nodes to become firmer, until they form a wedge between the bands. Such a condition prevents the bands from correct phonation and causes chronic hoarseness. The singer with nodes usually forces the voice, to overcome the obstacle, causing the condition to worsen. Nodes are cured by complete rest, permitting the bands to heal (much like callouses on the hands will heal). Nodes never develop if the singer takes good care of his voice and uses it correctly.

The larynx, which houses the vocal bands, is one of the most marvelous instruments in our body. It deserves good care, for it has many functions. First, it functions as an important part of the respiratory system, acting as a passageway for the ingress and egress of air. Second, it functions as a protective valve for the respiratory tract by keeping foreign matter out. If you have ever had food or water "go down the wrong way" you have discovered how important the larynx is, not only in keeping foreign matter out of the respiratory tract but in coughing it up when it does try to enter. Finally, the larynx acting as a valve *closes* the air passageway, thus trapping air in the lungs to prepare the thorax for body efforts. Persons who have had to have the larynx removed by surgery because of cancer not only lose the ability of normal speech but also find it difficult to lift heavy objects, blow their noses, or blow out a match, and they lose much of the sense of smell.

To see how the larynx looks, study Figure 7-1.

And take good care of your voice!

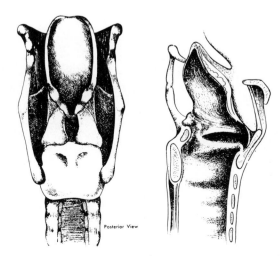

Posterior View

Figure 7-1
Larynx; Interior of Larynx

SONG INTERPRETATION AND MUSICIANSHIP

Amarilli, mia bella, *Caccini*

The tempo is marked *Moderato affetuoso,* which means "with moderate movement" (*moderato*) and with "tender, passionate expression" (*affetuoso*). The style of this song is very *legato*. Strive to connect the notes in long lines as you did with "Caro Mio Ben."

Measures 1-10: Sing as one long phrase within which there are three shorter phrases.

Measures 11-20: Feel these measures as dividing first into four bars, then two bars, then four more bars.

Measures 21-27: The composer has written a sequence, a series of ascending, repeated figures which lead to a climax.

Measures 28–32: The composer has written a *coda* (tail) for the song. Sing very freely, with great expression. Note that the song is written in a minor key. Figure out what the key is and what *kind* of minor it is.

On page 192 is another and highly contrasting song in a minor key, Beethoven's "Song of the Flea." Learn this song along with "Amarilli." Both are set in minor keys but are completely different in style and mood.

AMARILLI, MIA BELLA

Amarilli, My Fair One

Giulio Caccini
(1546–1614)

Moderato affettuoso

A - ma - ril - li, my fair one, O will you not be-
A - ma - ril - li, mia bel - la, Non cre - di, o del mio

lieve how_____ much I love you, And_____ how much_____
cor dol - ce, de - si - o, d'es - ser tu_____

_____ I a - dore you? With all my heart I pledge you
_____ l'a-mor mi - o? Cre - di - lo pur; e se ti-

you A - ma - ril - li, A - ma - ril - - -
re: A - ma - ril - li, A - ma - ril -

li, A - mà - ril li, I a - dore you! A - ma -
li, A - ma - ril - li, è il mio a - mo - re; A - ma -

ril - li,___ I a - dore _____ you! A - ma -
ril - li,___ è il mio a - mo - - - - re.

8

The $\overline{oo}$ Vowel

Webster: $\overline{oo}$
International: u

WORDS WITH THE $\overline{oo}$ VOWEL

Read aloud slowly:

soon	noon	prune	boom
cool	broom	to	lose
tool	plume	loom	loop
shoe	food	who	through

Sing.

1. Very slowly.

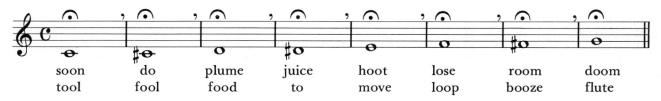

soon	do	plume	juice	hoot	lose	room	doom
tool	fool	food	to	move	loop	booze	flute

2. Very slowly.

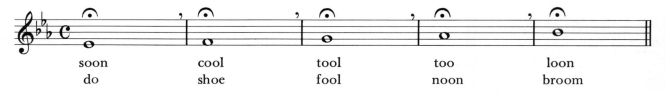

soon	cool	tool	too	loon
do	shoe	fool	noon	broom

3. Very slowly; sing with one breath.

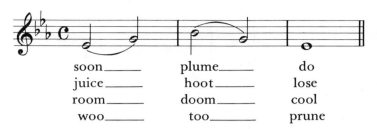

soon_____	plume_____	do
juice_____	hoot_____	lose
room_____	doom_____	cool
woo_____	too_____	prune

4. Moderately; sing with one breath.

soon_____	plume_____	hoot_____	room
cool_____	you_____	coo_____	mood
tool_____	food_____	move_____	booze
shoe_____	goose_____	soothe_____	brood

SENTENCES WITH THE $\overline{OO}$ VOWEL

Sing until all $\overline{OO}$ vowels are clearly executed.

1. Very slowly.

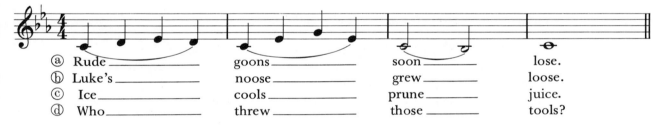

ⓐ Rude_____	goons_____	soon_____	lose.
ⓑ Luke's_____	noose_____	grew_____	loose.
ⓒ Ice_____	cools_____	prune_____	juice.
ⓓ Who_____	threw_____	those_____	tools?

2. Very slowly.

| ⓐ Brooms_ sweep_ court_ rooms. | ⓑ June_ plays_ that_ flute._ |
| ⓒ Do_ you_ like_ soup? | ⓓ Hugh_ likes_ black_ shoes._ |

3. Moderately.

ⓐ Rude_____ goons_ soon_ lose.
ⓑ Luke's_____ noose_ grew_ loose.
ⓒ Ice_____ cools_ prune_ juice.
ⓓ Who_____ threw_ those_ tools?

4. Sing with one breath.

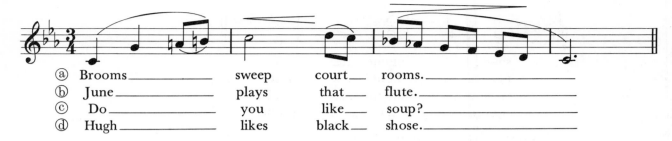

ⓐ Brooms_____	sweep	court__	rooms._____
ⓑ June_____	plays	that__	flute._____
ⓒ Do_____	you	like__	soup?_____
ⓓ Hugh_____	likes	black__	shose._____

STUDY

The $\overline{OO}$ ($\overline{oo}$) Vowel: Description and Execution

The $\overline{OO}$ vowel is the most closed of all vowels. It is the highest of all the dark, back vowels.

Sing $\overline{OO}$ as follows:

1. The back of the tongue is arched toward the soft palate.
2. The tip of the tongue touches the lower front teeth.
3. The lips are rounded forward to a small opening about the size of the tip of the little finger.

Keep the sides of the lips narrow so that they form a circle, not a slit. Do not pull the upper lip downward; allow it to protrude well away from the teeth.

The $\overline{OO}$ (u) Vowel: Common Faults and Corrections

Do not allow $\overline{OO}$ to sound "swallowed" or "hooty," a condition caused by opening the mouth too much, creating too high a proportion of resonance in the throat and chest. Round the lips forward, so that they are almost closed. Concentrate $\overline{OO}$ resonance in the mouth and head and nasal cavities.

General Principles of Singing

The $\overline{OO}$ vowel is an excellent sound for helping the male student to develop his *falsetto* voice. The term *falsetto* does not imply that this is an improper voice. *Falsetto* means simply a different *type* of voice from the normal, "full" male voice. When one sings *falsetto,* only the upper portion of the vocal bands phonate (look back at Fig. 1-7, *F*), and almost all resonance is in the head and nasal cavities. Moreover, the vocal bands are not completely closed, a position which gives the *falsetto* its soft, almost breathy quality. A smooth crescendo from *falsetto* to full voice is impossible because a "break" in the voice occurs when the vocal bands close.

The *falsetto* should be developed by the male singer, for it is valuable in singing passages of a high *tessitura*. In developing the *falsetto,* resonate a high proportion of tone at the hard palate and in the head and nasal cavities. There should be a sensation of "breathing into the tone." Learn to balance the breath allotted to the *falsetto,* so that the tone does not sound breathy. Male students should practice the following exercises daily until the *falsetto* voice is secured.

Caution: Always start *falsetto* development on extremely high notes and work down.

Sing at actual pitch.

Loo, Loo, Loo, Loo, Loo,   Loo, Loo, Loo, Loo, Loo,   Loo, Loo, Loo, Loo, Loo,   etc.

Loo, Loo, Loo, Loo, Loo,   Loo, Loo, Loo, Loo, Loo,   Loo, Loo, Loo, Loo, Loo,   etc.

Loo,   Loo,   Loo,   Loo,   etc.

SONG INTERPRETATION AND MUSICIANSHIP

Wanderer's Night Song, *Schubert*

The tempo is marked *lento,* which means "slowly." *Lento* is often used in music to indicate a temporary slowness. In this song, however, Schubert has used it to indicate the tempo throughout. The song should be sung with a feeling of restfulness and quiet.

The training text contains many words having the $\overline{OO}$ vowel.

Note that both staves of the accompaniment are in the bass clef.

There are many ♪ ♪ notes and 𝅘𝅥𝅭 𝅘𝅥𝅯 figures in this song. All too often, singers perform these sixteenth notes too rapidly, without giving them time to "sound." The end result is an unclear rendition that is often out of tune.

General Rule: Sing fast moving figures a bit slower if the style of the song permits. Allow fast moving notes to be heard.

Measure 4: Sustain the 𝅘𝅥𝅭 notes for their full value.

Measure 6: Sing the ♪ ♪ notes in correct rhythm.

Measure 8: The figure 𝅘𝅥𝅯𝅘𝅥𝅯 𝅘𝅥 𝅘𝅥𝅯𝅘𝅥𝅯 is a syncopation (a displacement of normal beat or accent).

General Rule: When learning songs that have rhythmic problems, speak the words first in correct rhythm, before singing. If you cannot speak the words in correct rhythm, you cannot sing them.

Measures 9-13: There are two phrases here that are exactly alike. They should be sung so that there is musical contrast. Observe the dynamic markings printed over these phrases, and the desired contrast will be attained.

Along with Schubert's slow, atmospheric song, see page 197 for Thomas Arne's "The Lass with the Delicate Air." Dr. Arne was an eighteenth-century English composer of great importance who wrote oratorios and many operas and other stage works. He wrote over twenty volumes of songs. Some sources credit him

77

as the first to use female voices in the oratorio chorus. (Soprano and alto parts were previously sung by boys.)

Sing "The Lass with the Delicate Air" gracefully and with good humor.

WANDERER'S NIGHT SONG

Wanderers Nachtlied

German text by Goethe

Franz Schubert

1. Training text: Soon the moon will shine through the
2. German text: Ü - ber al - len Gi - pfeln ist

trees, cool breez - es soft - ly waft the leaves,
Ruh', in al - len Gi - pfeln spü - rest du

call - ing to rest. Each tune - ful swall - ow
kaum ei - nen Hauch; die Vög - lein schwei - gen,

78

79

9

The *IH* and *EH* Vowels

Webster: ĭ and ĕ
International: ɪ and ɛ

WORDS WITH THE *IH* AND *EH* VOWELS

Read aloud slowly:

bid	sit	Ned	fed
kid	mid	west	lend
bit	miss	went	Bess
kit	pit	quest	end

Sing.

1. Very slowly.

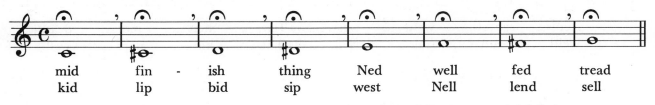

2. Very slowly.

3. Very slowly; sing with one breath.

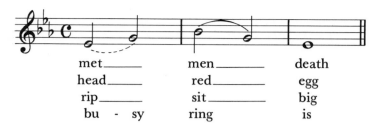

met	men	death
head	red	egg
rip	sit	big
bu - sy	ring	is

4. Moderately; sing with one breath.

bid	fin - ish	thing
Ned	well	fed	tread
kid	lip	mid	sip
west	Nell	lend	sell

SENTENCES WITH THE *IH* AND *EH* VOWELS

Sing until all *IH* and *EH* vowels are clearly executed.

1. Very slowly.

ⓐ Bring ____ this ____ quick - ly.
ⓑ Dance ____ with ____ Miss ____ Pitts.
ⓒ They ____ met ____ in ____ France.
ⓓ Which ____ is ____ named ____ Bess?

2. Very slowly.

ⓐ Ned's ___ guest ___ went ___ west. ___ ⓑ Ten ___ men ___ met ___ death!
ⓒ Well! ___ said ___ fair ___ Nell. ___ ⓓThat ___ kid ___ sings ___ well.

3. Moderately.

ⓐ Bring ____ this ___ quick - ly.
ⓑ Dance ____ with ___ Miss ___ Pitts.
ⓒ They ____ met ___ in ___ France.
ⓓ Which ____ is ___ named ___ Bess?

4. Sing with one breath.

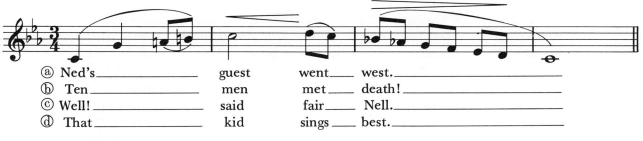

ⓐ Ned's_____ guest went_____ west._____
ⓑ Ten_____ men met_____ death!_____
ⓒ Well!_____ said fair_____ Nell._____
ⓓ That_____ kid sings_____ best._____

STUDY

The *IH* (ĭ) and *EH* (ĕ) Vowels: Description and Execution

The *IH* vowel is a closed, bright, front vowel and is executed as follows:

1. The front of the tongue is raised, but not so high as for *EE*.
2. The tip of the tongue is forward.
3. The upper lip is raised in a smiling position.
4. The jaw is dropped slightly to about the same position as for *EE*. *IH* and *EE* are the only front vowels that are closed.

The *EH* vowel is an open, bright, front vowel. *EH* is sung as follows:

1. The front of the tongue is raised, but not so high as for *IH*.
2. The tip of the tongue is forward.
3. The upper lip is raised in a smiling position.
4. The jaw is down in a relaxed position.

The *IH* (ɪ) and *EH* (ɛ) Vowels: Common Faults and Corrections

Singers substitute *IH* for *EH*. They sing *sinned* instead of *send, pin* for *pen, minny* for *many,* and *inny* for *any.* To avoid this, sing *IH* more closed than *EH.* Also, sing *IH* with the color of *EE, EH* with the color of *AY.*

Practice speaking and singing the following words in sequence:

	EE (i)	*IH* (ɪ)	*EH* (ɛ)	*AY* (eɪ)
	me	miss	met	may
	fee	fit	fell	fade
	be	bit	bed	base
	leap	lip	led	lake

Do not tense the lower lip, tighten the jaw, or pull at the corners of the mouth when singing *EH.* Simply drop the jaw in a relaxed, comfortable manner.

When singing final unstressed *y* or *ies,* do not sing *EE* or *EEz.* The vowel sound should be *IH.* This applies even when final *y* is rhymed with final *EE* as in "love*ly*" and "th*ee*," "myst*ery*" and "sl*ee*p," "melo*dy*" and "sh*e*." (NOTE: *y* is sometimes a diphthong, as in *my, thy,* and *sky.* See lesson 11.)

Practice speaking and singing the following words, which are pronounced with *IH:*

d*i*vine	w*i*nd (noun)
pr*e*tty	g*i*ve
b*u*sy	w*o*men
beaut*i*ful	rh*y*thm

General Principles of Singing

It was pointed out in lesson 2 that certain vowels are called "fundamental," while others are called "subordinate." The vowels *EE, AY, AH* (*farm*), *AW, OH,* and $\overline{OO}$ are fundamental. All other vowels are subordinate because they are considered modifications of the fundamental sounds. *EH* and *IH* are subordinate: *EH* is a modification of the fundamental *AY* vowel: *IH* is a modification of *EE.*

Figure 9-1 shows the relative tongue positions for each of the front vowels, from most closed to most open. Notice that for each vowel position, the tongue is forward, and the front is raised. In the next lesson, the other vowels will be similarly diagrammed.

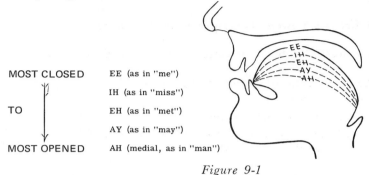

MOST CLOSED   EE (as in "me")

                IH (as in "miss")

TO   EH (as in "met")

                AY (as in "may")

MOST OPENED   AH (medial, as in "man")

Figure 9-1

SONG INTERPRETATION AND MUSICIANSHIP

Where'er You Walk, *Handel*

This song should be sung lyrically, with deep feeling. This is a love song, but do not sing it in the style of "popular" love songs. There should be a feeling of dignity and stateliness.

Memorize the following:

D.C. al Fine: D.C. means *da capo,* "from the beginning"; *al Fine* means "to the word *Fine"*

Adagio: slow. In the music of the eighteenth century, *adagio* is often used to indicate a temporary change to a slower tempo, as at cadences before repeats.

Measure 2: Do not sing the ♩♩ notes as ♩♩ notes.

Caution: Even though these notes move rapidly, give them time to be heard.

Measures 12-13: These are to be sung with one breath. The rests are observed by stopping the sound but not renewing the breath.

Measure 15: The long rests in this measure help to prepare the *adagio.* Make a slight *ritard* in measure 14. Give the quarter note ("sit") a bit more than its full value. Then, after a pause, sing the notes in measure 15 with a feeling of cadence.

At the time that Handel wrote his music, singers embellished songs as much as they desired. Composers allowed for this individuality by putting in long pauses, cadences, and indications where a cadenza would be most appropriate. Therefore, when singing this composition, mold your phrases and sing with a florid style.

The text of this song and fragments of the text are repeated with contrasting embellishments and florid treatment. It is this florid, irregular treatment which caused the name "baroque" to be given to the period in which this music was written.

There are two very important stylistic characteristics of the Baroque.

1. *Upbeat phrasing*. The Greek word *anacrusis* which means *upbeat* is often used to denote this kind of phrasing. It implies that phrasing is to be across the beat and across the bar. Some examples will serve to illustrate:

a.) 1. Upbeat Phrasing

2. Beat Phrasing

Note that in example a-1, the fourth beat is phrased across the bar to the first beat, and then the second, third, and fourth beats lead again across the bar to the next downbeat. In example a-2, stresses are on the first and third strong beats (like a march). These accents destroy any feel of upbeat phrasing.

b.) 1.

2.

In example b-1, the sixteenth notes are phrased so that the fourth in each group goes across the *beat* to the next group. In b-2, stress is on the first sixteenth in each group of four so that they are phrased *on* the beat, not *across* it.

c.) 1.

2.

Here again, in c-1, the triplets are phrased across the beat and across the bar, but in c-2, they are phrased *on* the beat.

These examples are a simplification of an important Baroque stylistic principle, for not only are notes phrased in this manner; entire measures often lead in upbeat form to other measures and entire phrases to other phrases. Sing each example on a neutral syllable until you feel the upbeat.

In Handel's "Where E'er You Walk" phrasing has been indicated above the voice line as follows: broken lines ⌒ indicate small note phrases; bold-face lines ⌒ indicate the larger phrases. Seek to bring to this song a feeling of the upbeat style. Avoid exaggeration. The great Baroque composers (Handel, Bach, Vivaldi, among others) built the style into their music. You have only to bring it out!

2. *Doctrine of Affects*. The aim of the Baroque composer was the expression of feelings or emotions, of "affects." Sacred music had to extol the "glory of God"; secular music had to contribute to the mind's "recreation." This "doctrine of affects" differed from later music primarily in degree. A Baroque piece sought to express a single basic affect, whereas a piece by Brahms, for example, might have dramatic changes in emotional content and feeling within a single work.

The Baroque composer, perhaps more than any other, created his affect through *tone painting*. Musical notes not only sounded like the "affect" being created; they often were made to *look* like it. A good example is the opening tenor aria in Handel's famous *Messiah*. After the recitative, "Comfort Ye," the tenor sings, "Every valley shall be exalted, the crooked [made] straight, and the rough places plain, and every mountain and hill made low." But look what Handel does with the notes!

Example 1: On the word "exalted" Handel has written an ascending sequence, thus lifting, raising, "exalting" the word both to the eye and to the ear.

Example 2: He builds a "mountain" with notes, then a smaller "hill," then a low note on the word "low."

Example 3: On the word "crooked" the notes are crooked, followed by a "straight" pitch.

Example 4: He obviously has "straightened out" the rough places and made them "plain."

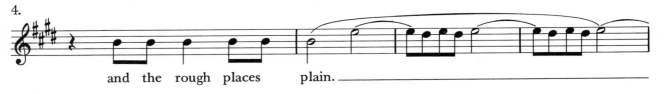

Always look for tone painting in Baroque and other music. Learn to see how the composer builds for "affect."

Another Baroque song which may be studied along with "Where E'er You Walk" is "Dido's Lament" by Henry Purcell. You will find this song on p. 202. Purcell was an early Baroque composer (*circa* 1658–1695) who wrote one of the truly great English masterworks, *Dido and Aeneas.* Study this song for its Baroque characteristics. Note that it is a lament. Notice how the piano introduction descends in gloomy half-steps until a full octave is reached. Note the minor key. Make certain that you phrase this song according to the Baroque principles that have been discussed.

This aria is from Semele, *one of the many operas written by Handel.*

WHERE E'ER YOU WALK

George F. Handel

to—— a shade.

Where e'er you tread, the blush-ing flow'r shall rise, And all things flour-ish, and all things flour-ish where e'er you turn your eyes, where e'er you turn your eyes, where e'er you turn your eyes.

Fine

89

10

The *UH* and Medial *OO* Vowels

Webster: ŭ and o͞o
International: ʌ and ʊ

WORDS WITH THE *UH* AND MEDIAL *OO* VOWELS

Read aloud slowly:

mum	fun	brook	good
hunt	sung	book	look
run	lump	took	full
sun	young	shook	would

Sing:

1. Very slowly.

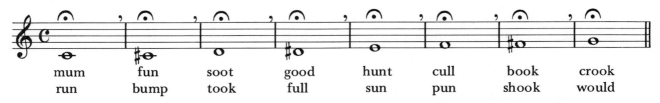

mum	fun	soot	good	hunt	cull	book	crook
run	bump	took	full	sun	pun	shook	would

2. Very slowly.

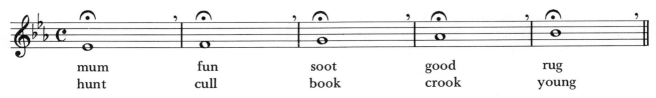

mum	fun	soot	good	rug
hunt	cull	book	crook	young

3. Very slowly; sing with one breath.

mum____	hunt____	run
sun____	bug____	rug
soot____	book____	took
shook____	wolf____	look

4. Moderately; sing with one breath.

mum____	fun____	soot____	good
hunt____	cull____	book____	crook
run____	bump____	took____	full
sun____	pun____	shook____	would

SENTENCES WITH THE *UH* AND MEDIAL *OO* VOWELS

Sing until all *UH* and medial *OO* vowels are clearly executed.

1. Very slowly.

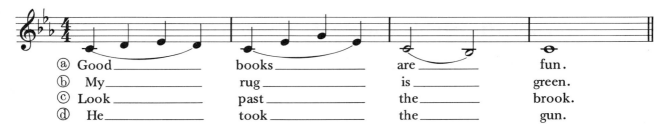

ⓐ Good____ books____ are ____ fun.
ⓑ My____ rug ____ is ____ green.
ⓒ Look____ past ____ the____ brook.
ⓓ He____ took____ the____ gun.

2. Very slowly.

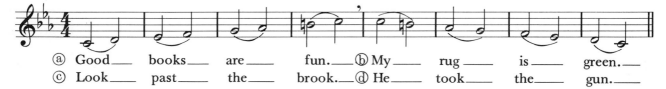

ⓐ Good__ books__ are__ fun.__ ⓑ My__ rug__ is__ green.__
ⓒ Look__ past__ the__ brook.__ ⓓ He__ took__ the__ gun.__

3. Moderately.

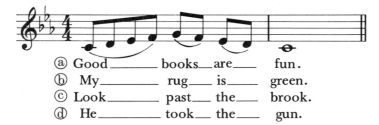

ⓐ Good____ books__ are__ fun.
ⓑ My____ rug__ is__ green.
ⓒ Look____ past__ the__ brook.
ⓓ He____ took__ the__ gun.

4. Sing with one breath.

ⓐ	Good_____	books	are ___	fun._____
ⓑ	My_____	rug	is ___	green._____
ⓒ	Look_____	past	the ___	brook._____
ⓓ	He_____	took	the ___	gun._____

STUDY

The *UH* (ŭ) and Medial *OO* (o͝o) Vowels: Description and Execution

The *UH* vowel is an open vowel. *UH,* a modification of fundamental *AH* (*farm*), is similar in quality and execution, but the tongue is in a slightly different position, and the jaw is not so low. Sing *UH* as follows:

1. The middle of the tongue is raised slightly.
2. The tip of the tongue is forward.
3. The lips are in a relaxed, neutral position.
4. The jaw is dropped in a relaxed position.

The medial *OO* vowel is an open vowel and is a modification of fundamental *OO* (*lose*). It is called "medial" to denote its place between fundamental *OO* and *OH* (*low*). Medial *OO* is sung as follows.

1. The middle of the tongue is raised higher than for *UH.*
2. The tip of the tongue is forward.
3. The lips are slightly rounded and protruded but must be relaxed in a neutral position.
4. The jaw is dropped in a relaxed position.

The *UH* (ʌ) and Medial *OO* (ʊ) Vowels: Common Faults and Corrections

The *UH* vowel is usually easy to sing. It appears infrequently and should never be sung except when appropriate, for undue use of this sound thickens and deadens the resonance of the voice. Clear execution of *UH* is very important. For example, in the prefix *un-, UH* must be distinct, for *un-* is a syllable that changes or denies the meaning of the word to which it is joined. Practice speaking and singing the following words.

*un*wise   *un*known   *un*kind   *un*sung

When singing medial *OO,* the rounding of the lips is larger than for fundamental *OO.* If the rounding is too small for medial *OO,* the sense of many words may be changed. Thus, *look* becomes *Luke, full* becomes *fool,* and *soot* becomes *suit.* Practice until there is a clear distinction between these sounds.

General Principles of Singing

With the conclusion of the present lesson, all eleven of the front, middle, and back vowels have been studied. In the previous lesson, a diagram of the positions of the front vowels was shown. Figure 10-1 shows the positions of the middle and back vowels.

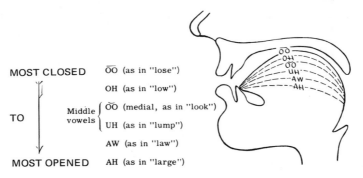

MOST CLOSED   O͞O (as in "lose")

                OH (as in "low")

TO   Middle vowels { O͝O (medial, as in "look")

                         UH (as in "lump")

                AW (as in "law")

MOST OPENED   AH (as in "large")

Figure 10-1

Note that the tip of the tongue remains forward for each of these vowels. Note also that the back or middle of the tongue is raised for each.

Two other vowel sounds remain to be studied:

1. *The weak vowel* (oc*ea*n). This vowel sound, which appears only in unstressed syllables, derives its name from its short, indefinite, obscure character. In each of the following words, a syllable with the weak vowel is in italics.

oc*ea*n	hand*some*	na*tion*	com*fort*
glad*ness*	trea*sure*	sad*ness*	*the* (before a consonant sound)
nev*er*	need*ed*	*of*	*a* (before a consonant sound)

The weak vowel appears so frequently in English that it is impossible to list all of its forms. Moreover, this vowel cannot be practiced as a separate, distinct sound detached from a word. It must be practiced only in its context. It must be executed with exactly the right duration and quality, for if it is given stress and is unduly prolonged,* diction sounds distorted and affected. Thus, "heed*ed*" becomes "he–*dead*," "of" becomes "*awv*," and "*the* boy" becomes "*thah* boy." Recognize this sound wherever it appears and produce it properly.

2. *The umlaut vowel* (b*i*rd). Although spelled in various ways, the umlaut vowel is always followed by the consonant *r*.

b*i*rd	b*u*rn	w*o*rd	t*u*rn	h*er*
l*ear*n	f*i*rm	y*ear*n	st*i*r	g*i*rl

There are two reasons for calling this sound the "umlaut vowel." First, it is almost the same as the German umlaut *o* (*ö*). Second, the word *umlaut* means "to change" (*um*) "the sound" (*laut*). Since this vowel has many spellings, it must literally be changed.

Sing the umlaut vowel with the lips curled forward like the bell of a horn. Retain this position up and down the scale, lowering the jaw as the voice goes higher. Soften *r* before a consonant sound. (See lesson 16.)

SONG INTERPRETATION AND MUSICIANSHIP

A Boat Song, *Grieg*

The tempo is marked *allegretto grazioso* which means "with some animation" (*allegretto*) in a "graceful style" (*grazioso*).

* Exceptions occur only when a composer has placed a single syllable with the weak vowel on a long, sustained note.

Measures 5-10: Execute the chord intervals without sliding from one note to another. The octave skip from measure 6 to 7 may be particularly awkward. Octaves are difficult to sing. Practice octaves up and down .the scale.

Measures 13-15: The descending chromatic passages sometimes present problems because of the tendency to space the descending intervals too low.

General Rule: When singing descending intervals, think of the interval as being smaller and closer to the one above. In ascending passages, think of the interval as being larger.

Measure 17: The key changes to E major. This is called a *modulation.*

Measures 17-22: Practice the expanding intervals as a separate exercise. Measures 17-18 have a skip of a third; 19-20, a skip of a fourth; 21, a skip of a fifth. To prepare for these intervals, use the following exercise in various keys. Use neutral syllables or a single vowel.

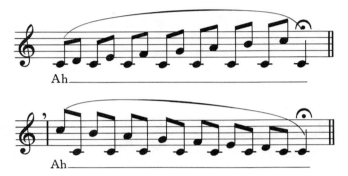

Measure 23: There is a modulation back to F major.
Double dots at double bar lines indicate that music in between is to be repeated. ‖: :‖ The first ending [1. 2. is sung at the end of all verses except the last. For the last verse, the second ending is used.

Look on page 205 for Roger Quilter's "O Mistress Mine," another song requiring a graceful, controlled style of singing. Quilter was born in England in 1877. He is known chiefly for his songs, most of which are graceful settings of English lyrics, many from Shakespeare. This particular song is in strophic form. Sing with warmth and tenderness.

Grieg's songs owe much of their popularity to the piquant and expressive melodic idioms which he borrowed from the folksongs of Norway. "A Boat Song" is inimitable in its charm and delicacy.

BOAT SONG

Im Kahne

Allegretto grazioso

Edvard Grieg
(1843—1907)

1. Sea - gulls, sea - gulls a - bove are flock - ing in bright _____ sun - shine;
2. Loos - en, loos - en, my love, thy hood _____ o'er tress - es bright;
3. Rock me rock me, O gen - tle rip - plets from _____ the sea;

Each lit - tle gos - ling with yel - low stock - ings clear and fine;
Then we will dance in the warm and shin - ing moon - lit night;
Fair my___ love, as a young fawn slend - er, comes to me;

Row, row, to Fish - er's strand, all is calm as we
Wait! wait! we must de - lay, There'll be danc - ing on
Rock, rock in dreams di - vine, I am thine and___

near the land, Seas are ly - ing so still, Oh!
wed - ding day, Fid - dles play - ing their fill, Oh!
thou art mine, Vi - o - lins now are still, Oh!

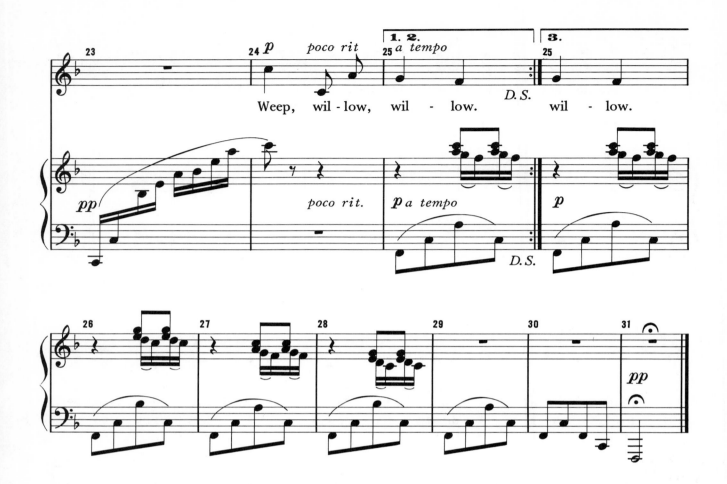

Weep, wil - low, wil - low.   wil - low.

11

The AY͡-ĬH, OH͡-ŎŎ, and AH͡-ĬH Diphthongs

Webster: ā, ō, and ī
International: eɪ, oʊ, and aɪ

WORDS WITH THE *AY͡-ĬH, OH͡-ŎŎ,* AND *AH͡-ĬH* DIPHTHONGS

Read aloud slowly:

may	say	oh	blow	I	might
pay	praise	no	row	my	ride
play	aid	snow	throw	why	chime
lay	day	so	flow	die	find

Sing.

1. Very slowly.

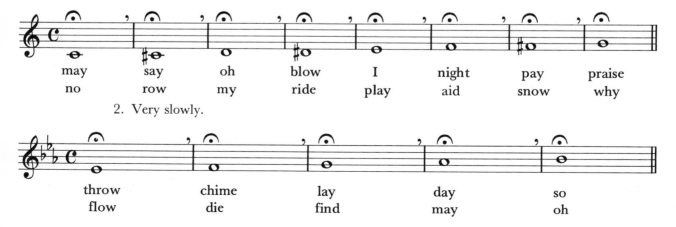

100

3. Very slowly; sing with one breath.

may_____	say_____	pay
no_____	oh _____	throw
night_____	my_____	I
lay_____	throw_____	why

4. Moderately; sing with one breath.

may_____	say_____	pay_____	praise
no_____	oh_____	row_____	snow
my_____	night_____	I_____	why
lay_____	flow_____	find_____	day

SENTENCES WITH THE *AY͡-IH*, *OH͡-O͝O*, AND *AH͡-IH* DIPHTHONGS

Sing until all diphthongs are clearly executed.

1. Very slowly.

ⓐ They_____	may_____	play_____	games.
ⓑ "Oh_____	no,"_____	moaned_____	Joe.
ⓒ Ice_____	shines_____	by_____	night
ⓓ The_____	light_____	has_____	blown.

2. Very slowly.

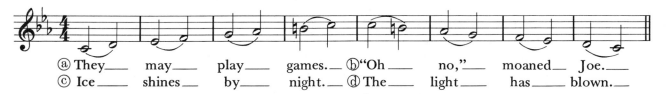

| ⓐ They___ | may___ | play___ | games. | ⓑ"Oh ___ | no," ___ | moaned ___ | Joe. ___ |
| ⓒ Ice___ | shines___ | by___ | night.___ | ⓓ The ___ | light___ | has___ | blown.___ |

3. Moderately.

ⓐ They_____	may___	play___	games.
ⓑ "Oh_____	no,"___	moaned	Joe.
ⓒ Ice_____	shines___	by___	night.
ⓓ The_____	light___	has___	blown.

4. Sing with one breath.

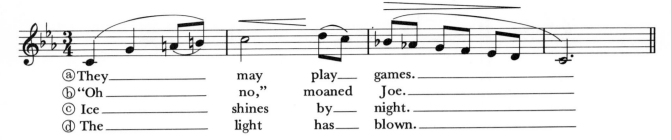

ⓐ They_____ may play__ games._____
ⓑ "Oh _____ no," moaned Joe._____
ⓒ Ice_____ shines by__ night._____
ⓓ The_____ light has__ blown._____

STUDY

The *AY-IH* (ā), *OH-OO* (ō), and *AH-IH* (ī) Diphthongs: Description and Execution

A diphthong is a syllable which combines two vowel sounds. The word *diphthong* (pronounced "dif-thong") is derived from the Greek *di-*(*twice*) and *phthongos* (*sounds*). In all diphthongs, one of the vowel sounds is stressed and sustained; the other is unstressed and short. The two vowel sounds are referred to as (1) the sustained sound, and (2) the vanishing sound.

The diphthong *AY-IH* combines two front, bright vowel sounds. *AY* (*may*) is the sustained sound; *IH* (*miss*) is the vanishing sound. Refer to lesson 3 for a description of *AY* and to lesson 9 for *IH*.

The diphthong *OH-OO* combines two back, dark vowel sounds. *OH* (*obey*) is the sustained sound; *OO* (*look*) is the vanishing sound. Refer to lesson 7 for *OH*, and to lesson 10 for *OO*.

The diphthong *AH-IH* combines two front, bright vowel sounds. *AH* (*and*) is the sustained sound; *IH* (*miss*) is the vanishing sound. Refer to lesson 5 for *AH* and to lesson 9 for *IH*.

The *AY-IH* (eɪ), *OH-OO* (oʊ), and *AH-IH* (aɪ) Diphthongs: Common Faults and Corrections

Avoid distorting one of the vowels in a diphthong. Some singers are oblivious to this fault until corrected. They sing *geh-oh* for *go*, or *toh-ihm* for *time*. Understand the form of a diphthong and avoid this mistake.

Do not omit the second sound in a diphthong. It must be articulated clearly if a word is to make sense.

An important principle to remember about diphthongs is that only *one* of the vowel sounds is sustained and stressed. Do not copy the crooner of popular music, for he often distorts the time values of diphthongs in order to achieve intimacy of style, an acceptable technique for only popular music.

The following shows the relative time values for each of the two vowels in the word *night:*

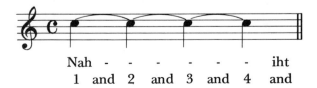

Nah - - - - - iht
1 and 2 and 3 and 4 and

The *AH* sound is sustained until after the fourth count, at which time *IH,* the vanishing sound, is briefly articulated.

Do not change the second vowel in *AY-IH* to *EE.* When this is done, *grace* sounds like *grease, may* like *me,* and *say* like *see.* Sing *IH* clearly.

Stressed *o* is pronounced as a diphthong (see lesson 8), but some students substitute *AW* for the diphthong, omitting the second sound (*OO*) entirely. They sing "*Gaw* 'way from my wind*aw*" and "*law* how a *rawz.* . . ." Learn to recognize both of the vowels in a diphthong, and pronounce each correctly.

SONG INTERPRETATION AND MUSICIANSHIP

Sapphic Ode, *Brahms*

This song should be sung slowly but with movement. Do not drag. The syncopated accompaniment provides underlying movement. The term *mezzo voce* means to use only half (*mezzo*) the power of the voice (*voce*).

In studying diphthongs in this work, at first isolate the sounds by circling words containing them. Underneath these diphthongs, write lightly, in pencil, the sustained sound in capital letters and the vanishing sound in small letters, as:

"Ro - ses	I	at	Night"
ROH-oo	AH-ih		NAH-iht

The sustained sound is thereby highlighted. Later, erase the pencil markings.

Review songs covered in previous lessons, analyzing the three diphthongs presented in this lesson. As other diphthongs are introduced, restudy in similar fashion.

This song has changes of measure length. Retain the half note throughout as the unit of beat. Note how the double bar (‖) indicates that a change is to occur.

Another song with many diphthongs is Edward Purcell's "Passing By," which you will find on page 208. Edward Purcell was the brother of Henry Purcell (who wrote "Dido's Lament"). This song, in strophic form, should be sung quite simply but with expression. Note that the first verse seeks to tell the audience a story; the second verse is more intimate, more personal; and the third is declamatory. Note, too, that after a four-bar introduction, the song is sixteen bars long. You should feel the melody in four-bar phrases, but make each four-bar phrase relate to the next so that all sixteen bars unfold as a unified melody.

There is hardly a singer of the present day who does not include some songs of Brahms in his repertory. Many of Brahms' songs are based on German folk songs which he collected and edited.

SAPPHIC ODE

Hans Schmidt

Johannes Brahms
(1833–1897)

1. Training text: Ro - ses I at night from the hedge - rows sev - ered, Sweet - er was their scent than in day - time ev - er; Yet the trem - bling branch - es so soft - ly

2. German text: Ro - sen brach ich nachts mir am dunk - len Ha - ge; sü - sser hauch - ten Duft sie, als je____ am Ta - ge, doch ver - streu - ten reich die be - weg - ten

* *Sapphic refers to Sappho, a poetess famous for her love lyrics.*

mov - ing, drops _____ were be - dew - ing.
Ae - ste Thau, _____ der mich näss - te.

E - ven so thy
Auch der küs - se

kiss - es my heart hath shak - en, Kiss - es that at
Duft mich wie nie be - rück - te, die ich nachts vom

night from thy lips___ I've ta - ken: Yet thou
Strauch dei -ner Lip - pen pflück - te: *doch auch*

too were trem-bling and soft - ly mov - ing,   Tear - - drops be -
dir, be -wegt im Ge -müth gleich je - nen,   *thau - - ten die*

dewed___ thee.
Thrä - - nen.

12

The *AH-OO̅O̅*, *AW-IH*, and *IH-OO̅O̅* Diphthongs

Webster: ou, oi, and iu
International: aʊ, ɔɪ, and ɪu

WORDS WITH THE *AH-OO̅O̅*, *AW-IH*, AND *IH-OO̅O̅* DIPHTHONGS

Read aloud slowly:

vow	out	voice	choice	view	new
cow	round	poise	Roy	due	mute
how	bow	noise	boy	few	pew
shout	now	joy	toy	cute	hue

Sing.

1. Very slowly.

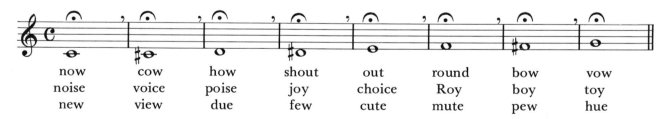

now	cow	how	shout	out	round	bow	vow
noise	voice	poise	joy	choice	Roy	boy	toy
new	view	due	few	cute	mute	pew	hue

2. Very slowly.

now	cow	how	round	bow
noise	joy	choice	boy	voice
new	due	few	mute	hue

3. Very slowly; sing with one breath.

now	how	round
noise	joy	boy
new	few	mute
bow	voice	due

4. Moderately; sing with one breath.

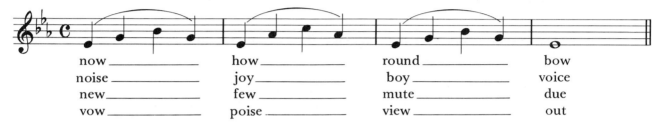

now	how	round	bow
noise	joy	boy	voice
new	few	mute	due
vow	poise	view	out

SENTENCES WITH *AH-OO̬*, *AW-IH*, AND *IH-OO̬* DIPHTHONGS

Sing until all diphthongs are clearly executed.

1. Very slowly.

ⓐ How_____ now_____ brown_____ cow?
ⓑ Choice_____ toys _____ bring _____ joy.
ⓒ New _____ views _____ a - muse.
ⓓ Dance_____ 'round _____ and_____ 'round.

2. Very slowly.

ⓐ How___ now___ brown___ cow?___ ⓑChoice___ toys___ bring___ joy.___
ⓒ New___ views___ a - muse.___ ⓓDance___'round___ and___ 'round.___

3. Moderately.

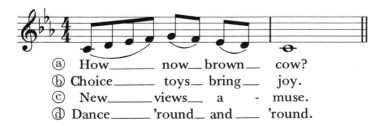

ⓐ How_____ now___brown___ cow?
ⓑ Choice_____ toys___ bring___ joy.
ⓒ New_____ views___ a - muse.
ⓓ Dance_____ 'round___ and _____ 'round.

4. Sing with one breath.

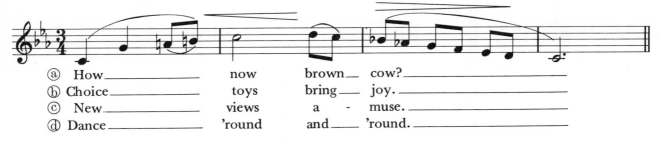

ⓐ How_____ now brown__ cow?_____
ⓑ Choice_____ toys bring__ joy. _____
ⓒ New_____ views a - muse._____
ⓓ Dance_____ 'round and____ 'round. _____

STUDY

The *AH-ŎO* (ou), *AW-IH* (oi), and *IH-ŌO* (iu) Diphthongs: Description and Execution

The diphthong *AH-ŎO* combines two back, dark vowels. *AH* (*large*) is the sustained sound; *ŎO* (*look*) is the vanishing sound. Refer to lesson 4 for a description of *AH,* and to lesson 10 for *ŎO*.

The diphthong *AW-IH* combines one back vowel and one front vowel. *AW* (*call*) is the sustained vowel; *IH* (*miss*) is the vanishing vowel. Refer to lesson 6 for a description of *AW,* and to lesson 9 for *IH*.

The diphthong *IH-ŌO* combines one front vowel and one back vowel. *IH* (*miss*) is the *vanishing* sound; *ŌO* (*lose*) is the *sustained* sound. Refer to lesson 9 for *IH* and to lesson 8 for *ŌO*. *IH-ŌO* is the only diphthong in which the second vowel is the sustained sound.

The *AH-ŎO* (aʊ), *AW-IH* (ɔɪ), and *IH-ŌO* (ɪʊ) Diphthongs: Common Faults and Corrections

AH-ŎO: Avoid singing *OH* instead of *AH* as in *no* for *now,* and *hoe* for *how.* "Think" fundamental *AH*. Do not round the lips forward. Drop the jaw and permit the upper front teeth to show. Note that the vanishing sound in this diphthong is *ŎO* (*look*), not *ŌO* (*move*).

AW-IH: Avoid singing *AH* for *AW* in this diphthong. Round the lips forward in an oval shape; otherwise you will sing *buy* for *boy,* and *tie* for *toy.* Do not omit the second vowel, or *poise* becomes *paws,* and *joy* becomes *jaw.*

IH-ŌO: Articulate the first vowel, or *due* will sound like *do,* and *mute* like *moot.* Sing the sustained sound as *ŌO* (*move*), not *ŎO* (*look*).

Singing diphthongs requires movement by the articulators from one vowel position to another. This movement must take place without any break in the tonal line, even when moving from a dark to a bright vowel, or from a front to a back vowel. The change must be made smoothly in a kind of "tonal glide." Avoid tension in the organs of articulation by relaxing the throat, tongue, jaw, and lips. Support and energize tones by correct breathing and breath control.

SONG INTERPRETATION AND MUSICIANSHIP

Bendemeer's Stream, *Irish Folk Song*

Sing in a graceful, lyrical fashion, avoiding heaviness. The words are narrative. Seek to tell a story.

The abbreviation *ten.* (*tenuto*) means "to hold," to sustain beyond full value.

One of the difficulties in singing a song of this type is to retain the folk-like simplicity while maintaining interest. Over-blown dramatics or excessive *rubato* are incorrect. All effects must be subtle.

This is a strophic setting, characteristic of folk songs. Strophic settings, because there is no harmonic and melodic difference for each verse, are difficult to perform expressively. Thus, performance requires great imagination and subtle variety.

On page 210 may be found a song written for this book by the American composer Wallace DePue. "Little Lamb" is a setting of William Blake's poem—and should be sung simply and reflectively. Dr. DePue is Coordinator of Theory in the School of Music at Bowling Green State University.

This famous folk song tells of the beauties of Bendemeer's Stream.

BENDEMEER'S STREAM

Irish Folk Song

Thomas Moore
(1779—1852)

Andante

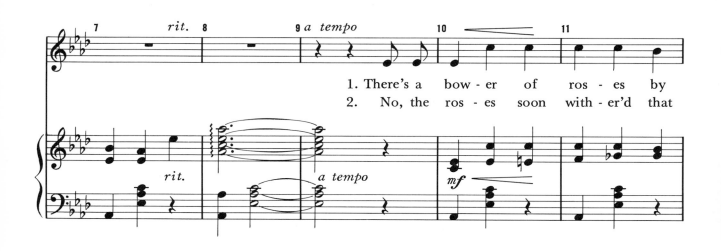

1. There's a bow - er of ros - es by
2. No, the ros - es soon with - er'd that

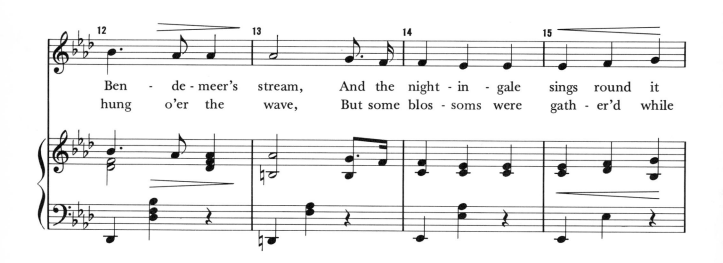

Ben - de-meer's stream, And the night - in - gale sings round it
hung o'er the wave, But some blos - soms were gath - er'd while

all the day long. In the time of my child-hood 'twas
fresh - ly they shone. And a dew was dis - till'd from their

like a sweet dream, To___ sit in the ros - es and
flow - ers that gave All the fra - grance of sum - mer when

hear the bird's song. That bow'r and its mus - ic I
sum - mer was gone. Thus mem - o - ry draws from de -

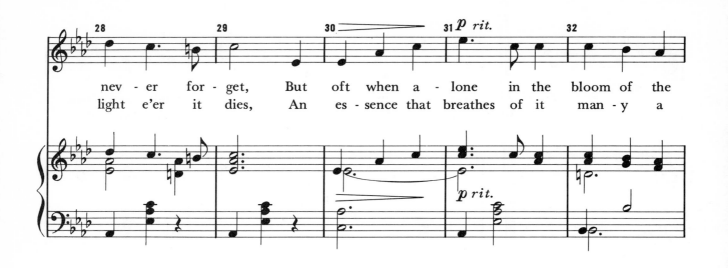

never for-get, But oft when a - lone in the bloom of the
light e'er it dies, An es - sence that breathes of it man - y a

year, I think: "Is the night - in - gale sing - ing there
year, Thus joy to my soul, as 'twas then to my

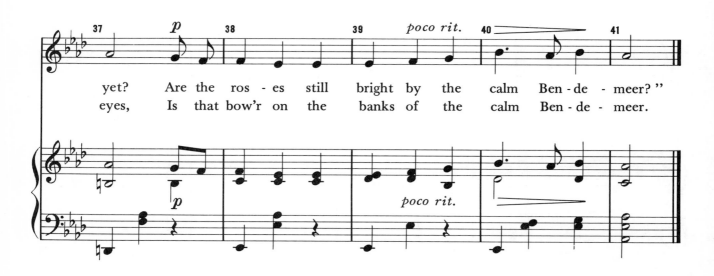

yet? Are the ros - es still bright by the calm Ben - de - meer?"
eyes, Is that bow'r on the banks of the calm Ben - de - meer.

13

Consonants Articulated with the Lips

Webster: b, p, m, hw, w
International: b, p, m, hw, w

WORDS WITH THE LIP CONSONANTS

Read aloud slowly:

bop	past	mop	when	wasp
Bob	pop	mob	whip	warm
bum	pent	Mom	which	way
bow	prove	mean	what	want

Sing.*

1.

bop__ Bob__ bum__ bow__   past__ pop__ pent__ way__   wand
mop__ mob__ mom__ when__   whip__ wasp__ want__ bop__   Bob

2.

bop_____ Bob_____ bum_____ bow_____   past_____ pop_____ prove_____ mop
warm_____ way_____ wand_____ bop_____   past_____ mop_____ when_____ wasp

* Lesson 13 introduces flexibility studies. They should be practiced first using vowels and neutral syllables. When they can be sung with reasonable control, the consonant study should be applied.

116

mop	mom	moan	when	whip	which	what	wasp
Bob	pop	mob	whip	warm	bum	pent	mom

3.

bop	Bob	bum	bow	past	pop	pent	prove
way	mud	win	wasp	warm	why	word	bring

mop	mob	mom	moan	whim	whip	which	what
pint	when	by	pose	mill	week	bunch	man

4.

bop	Bob	bum	bow	past	pop	pent	prove
mop	mob	mom	moan	when	whip	which	what
wasp	warm	way	ward	bunch	pint	mud	whim

SENTENCES WITH THE LIP CONSONANTS

Sing until all lip consonants are correctly executed.

1.

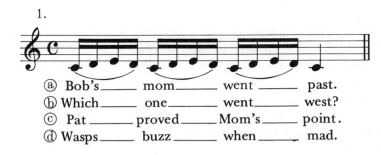

Ⓐ Bob's___ mom___ went ___ past.
Ⓑ Which___ one___ went___ west?
Ⓒ Pat ___ proved ___ Mom's ___ point.
Ⓓ Wasps___ buzz ___ when ___ mad.

2.

Ⓐ Bob's ___ mom ___ went ___ past.
Ⓑ Which ___ one ___ went ___ west?
Ⓒ Pat___ proved ___ Mom's ___ point. ___
Ⓓ Wasps___ buzz ___ when ___ mad. ___

3.

ⓐ Bob's _____ mom _____ went _____ past. _____
ⓑ Which _____ one _____ went _____ west? _____
ⓒ Pat _____ proved _____ Mom's _____ point. _____
ⓓ Wasps _____ buzz _____ when _____ mad. _____

4.

ⓐ Bob's _____ mom _____ went _____ past.
ⓑ Which _____ one _____ went _____ west?
ⓒ Pat _____ proved _____ Mom's _____ point.
ⓓ Wasps _____ buzz _____ when _____ mad.

STUDY

The Lip Consonants (b, p, m, hw, w): Description and Execution

Consonants are obstructions which appear before, between, and after vowels, giving meaning to the vowels. For example, a combination of the vowels medial *AH* and *IH* produces the pronoun *I* (*AH-IH*); an *n* before and a *t* after these vowels produces the noun *night* (*N-AH-IH-T*), a *b* before these vowels produces the verb *buy* (*B-AH-IH*); a *c* after these vowels produces the noun *ice* (*AH-IH-C*).

There are four general classifications of consonants:

Voiced consonants are those which cause vibration in the vocal bands. To feel these vibrations, place your hand, palm down, on the top of your head and sing *b, b, b.*

Voiceless consonants are those which do not cause vibration in the vocal bands. Place your hand, palm down, on the top of your head and sing *p, p, p.* Note that there is no vibration, only a puff of air. (There is, of course, vibration from the *EE* vowel which follows.)

Stop-plosive consonants are those which have no sustained sound and are followed by a puff of breath. Sing *p, p, p.* Note that this consonant is of short duration and cannot be sustained. It is, therefore, called "stopped," which means that a complete closure, or stoppage, of the nasal and oral passages takes place. Note, also, the sudden release of breath. It is, therefore, called "plosive," a word which has been extracted from *explosion* and *implosion* and means "the percussive shutting off or release of breath."

Continuant consonants have a sustained sound. Sing *m, m, m.* Note that the nasal passages are open and the sound can be held. It is, therefore, continuant, not plosive, in character.

Consonants are articulated in six different places. These are:

1. The lips (first place of articulation)

2. The lower lip and upper front teeth (second place)
3. The tip of the tongue (third place)
4. The tongue and the gum (fourth place)
5. The tongue and the palate (fifth place)
6. The back of the tongue (sixth place)

The consonants *b, p, m,* and *hw* are articulated as follows:

B(b): the lips are pressed lightly together, then parted suddenly by the emission of the voice. The tip of the tongue is forward; *b* is a voiced, stop-plosive consonant.

P(p): the lips are pressed lightly together, then parted suddenly by the emission of the breath. The tongue is forward; *p* is a voiceless, stop-plosive consonant.

M(m): the lips are pressed lightly together while the voice is emitted through the nose. The tongue is forward; *m* is a voiced, continuant consonant.

HW(hw): the lips are rounded easily forward while the breath is emitted through the mouth. After the emission of breath, there is a sudden change of the lips to form whatever vowel position follows; *hw* is a voiceless consonant, articulated with the sound of *h*. Any consonant of which *h* is a part is called an "aspirate." *Aspirate,* used as a verb, means "to pronounce with audible breath." There are two important rules concerning the aspirate:

1. When singing the aspirate, the emission of breath ceases instantly with the production of the vowel that follows.
2. The aspirate is always articulated with the mouth shaped for the vowel that follows. For example, sing *he* with the mouth shaped for *EE, hate* with the mouth shaped for *AY,* and *hand* with the mouth shaped for medial *AH.*

Read the following aloud; then sing, using the exercises at the beginning of this lesson.

he   hot   whose   hit   hand   heed   hop   hoop   how   have
  a) Who has his hoe?
  b) Her hair is white.
  c) What do they have?

W(w) is articulated as follows: The lips are rounded easily forward; the voice is emitted through the mouth. The tongue is forward; *w* at the beginning of a word is a voiced, continuant consonant. It is identical in execution to the *OO* (*move*) vowel but is considered a consonant because the lips widen suddenly to sing whatever vowel follows. At the end of a word, *w* has the character of a vowel (*how, now, cow*). Sometimes *w* is silent, as in *wring, wrong,* and *wrath.*

The Lip Consonants (b, p, m, hw, w): Common Faults and Corrections

The most common fault in singing lip consonants is tension in the lips. Relaxed lips result in clearly articulated consonants that can be heard and understood. Tense lips obscure and muddle the diction. They cause constriction in the throat. Practice speaking and singing the lip consonants with lips so relaxed that they feel flabby and rubberlike. When the lips are completely relaxed, the throat tends to be relaxed and the tone is clear, the diction understandable. Master the principle of relaxed lips before proceeding to the next lesson.

To sing the consonants:

B: do not protrude the lips or press them tightly together. Do not substitute *m* for *b* (sounding as though you have a cold). Note that in words ending in *mb, b* is silent (*climb, thumb, limb*). Do not sing a nonexistent *m* when *b* begins a word (*m*-because, *m*-beautiful). Sing *b* clearly in *pp* passages. When *b* occurs before a consonant sound or a stop (rest, breathing place, dramatic pause), it is followed by the vowel sound *UH*. When *UH* is not audible, *b* is also inaudible. For example:

job   must be sung as   jo - buh

Caution: Sing *UH* on exactly the same pitch as *b*.

P: relax the lips. Do not press them tightly together. Note that *p* and *b* are similarly executed. Do not sing: "My *bent*-up (pent-up) emotions," and "Let us *bray* (pray)." Remember that *p* is *not* voiced.

P is difficult to articulate when it precedes *t* as in *capture, rapture,* and *scripture*. Practice singing these words by over-aspirating the *p* consonant. Similarly, over-aspirate *p* before any consonant sound.

M: do not tighten the lips. They should be relaxed and barely touching. *M* (and *n*) are humming consonants which, when properly executed, can give smoothness, expressiveness, and resonance to singing. They can help to avoid note singing and to facilitate phrase singing by providing connection between vowels and words. For example, sing *O moon* and *Come to me:*

Ommm - ooon   Commm - tommm - ee

Note that *m* takes part of the time from the preceding vowel.

Caution: When *m* occurs between two vowels of different pitch

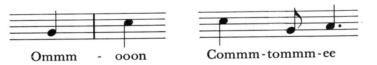

Ommm - ooon   Commm - tommm - ee

it is sung on the pitch of the first vowel *only,* regardless of which is the higher or lower. *Do not sing* m *on the second pitch or on both pitches.*

When *m* follows a consonant sound, do not attempt to prolong it, for there is no time for anticipation (*that mob, his mother*). When *m* precedes a consonant sound or a stop, it is prolonged, but another vowel should not be inserted. ("The thirst that *from - uh* the soul doth rise"; "Going *home - uh,* going *home - uh.*") Sing *m* by keeping the lips closed until the next consonant is sounded.

Hw and *w:* do not let the $\overline{OO}$ vowel become a part of *hw*. The lips are shaped for $\overline{OO}$, but breath, not tone, is sent through the lips. When *w* begins a word, there is an $\overline{OO}$ sound, but the lips must move quickly to the vowel that follows. Do not confuse *hw* and *w* by singing *witch* for *which,* and *wear* for *where.* Remember that *hw* is aspirated, *w* is voiced.

SONG INTERPRETATION AND MUSICIANSHIP

If Thou Be Near, *Bach*

This selection calls for a *legato* style. Establish *legato* by singing a phrase on a single vowel; then repeat the phrase with words, retaining the "connected" feeling. Thus, measures 5-8 would first be practiced:

Mah _____   Mah _____

Certain consonants, such as *m* and *n,* help to produce sustained sound. Search for these consonants throughout the song, and use them to secure a better *legato.*

Note that "If Thou Be Near" is a composition from the Baroque period. Review in lesson 9 how to approach upbeat *anacrusis* phrasing. Bring those principles to this song.

On page 212 is a fine song for male voice by the English composer Ralph Vaughan Williams. "The Vagabond" is the first of nine Stevenson songs which the composer published under the title *Songs of Travel.* The entire cycle is worthy of study and fun to sing.

Bach is considered by many to be one of the greatest composers of all time. His musical output was astounding, in terms of both quantity and quality, yet the song, "If Thou Be Near," which was dedicated to his wife, is the only love song that he wrote. Avail yourself of the opportunity to hear other compositions by Bach.

IF THOU BE NEAR

Bist Du Bei Mir

Johann Sebastian Bach
(1685—1750)

1.*Training text:* If thou be near, then I wait calm - ly

2.*German text:* Bist du bei mir, geh' ich mit Freu - den

to greet__ my__ death with grate - ful__ heart, to__

zum Ster - ben__ und zu mei - ner__ Ruh', zum__

then I wait calm - ly, to greet_ my_ death with grate -ful_
*geh' ich mit Freu - den, zum Ster - ben_ und zu mei -ner_*

heart, to _____ greet my death with grate -ful heart.
Ruh', zum _____ Ster - ben und zu mei - ner Ruh'!

14

Consonants Articulated with the Lower Lip and Upper Teeth

Webster: **f, v**
International: **f, v**

WORDS WITH THE LIP-TEETH CONSONANTS

Read aloud slowly:

fit	food	vow	grieve	fill	soft	view	brave
fall	oft	vast	voice	fair	laugh	verse	of

Sing:

fill _____ fair _____ soft _____ laugh _____ view _____ verse _____ brave _____ of

3.

fit _____ fill _____ fall _____ fair _____ food _____ soft _____ off _____ laugh

vow _____ view _____ vast _____ verse _____ grieve _____ brave _____ voice _____ of

4.

fit _____ fill _____ fall _____ fair _____ food _____ soft _____ off _____ laugh

vow _____ view _____ vast _____ verse _____ grieve _____ have _____ voice _____ of

SENTENCES WITH THE LIP-TEETH CONSONANTS

Sing until all consonants are clearly executed.

1.

ⓐ Ralph _____ fought _____ Jeff _____ Ford.
ⓑ Soft _____ laughs _____ foil _____ fear.
ⓒ Vines _____ freeze _____ from _____ frost.
ⓓ Love _____ vows _____ oft' _____ fail.

2.

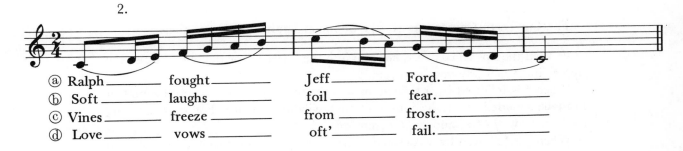

ⓐ Ralph _____ fought _____ Jeff _____ Ford.
ⓑ Soft _____ laughs _____ foil _____ fear. _____
ⓒ Vines _____ freeze _____ from _____ frost. _____
ⓓ Love _____ vows _____ oft' _____ fail. _____

3.

ⓐ Ralph___ fought___ Jeff___ Ford.___ ⓑ Soft___ laughs___ foil___ fear.___
ⓒ Vines___ freeze___ from___ frost.___ ⓓ Love___ vows___ oft'___ fail.___

4.

ⓐ Ralph_____ fought_____ Jeff_____ Ford.
ⓑ Soft_____ laughs_____ foil_____ fear.
ⓒ Vines_____ freeze_____ from_____ frost.
ⓓ Love_____ vows_____ oft'_____ fail.

STUDY

The Lip-Teeth Consonants (f, v): Description and Execution

F(f), a voiceless continuant, is articulated as follows:

1. The inside of the lower lip touches the upper front teeth.
2. While this position is held, the breath is emitted through the mouth.
3. The tip of the tongue is forward.

Articulate *V*(v), a voiced continuant, as follows:

1. The lower lip touches the upper front teeth.
2. While this position is held, the voice is emitted through the mouth.
3. The tongue is forward.

F and *V* are articulated in the same place and in the same manner; both are continuants. They differ in that *f* is voiceless and *v* is voiced. Many consonants are similar. Learn to recognize the distinctive characteristics of each. Ask the following questions about each consonant:

1. *Where* is it articulated?
2. *How* is it articulated?
3. Is it *voiced* or *voiceless?*

The Lip-Teeth Consonants (f, v): Common Faults and Corrections

F: keep the lips relaxed. Do not bite into the lower lip or tighten it. Raise the upper lip. Avoid any vocalized sound.

When *f* is followed by a syllable or a word beginning with a vowel sound, it must be sounded at the beginning of that syllable or word. For example, sing *o - ften,** not *of - ten,* and *a - ffair,* not *aff - air.*

When *f* is followed by a consonant, the vowel preceding *f* should be sustained

* The *t* in *often* is silent.

for its full duration, with *f* executed just before the consonant. For example, sing *if thou* as *i - fthou,* and *safe passage* as *sa - fepassage.*

When *f* occurs at the end of a word, do not add a vowel (*safe - uh, grief - uh*). Avoid this by keeping the lower lip and upper teeth together until the breath for *f* has been stopped.

V: the common faults in singing *f* also apply to *v.* The point of contact between the lower lip and upper teeth for singing *v* differs with people because facial structure, size, and shape of lips and teeth differ. Find the point of contact that produces a relaxed, resonant *v.* Do not tense the lips.

When *v* occurs between two vowel sounds of the same pitch, it should be connected to the first. Sing *viv - id,* not *vi - vid,* and *ev - il,* not *e - vil.* When *v* occurs between two vowel sounds of different pitches, it is always sung on the lower pitch:

vi - <u>v</u>id   e<u>v</u> - il

Caution: Do not scoop or slide. Sing *v* only on the lower pitch.

When *v* occurs at the end of a word before a stop or another word beginning with a consonant, do not allow an *uh* to sound (I *love - uh* you, *leave - uh* me). Stop the voice before the lower lip and upper teeth separate.

SONG INTERPRETATION AND MUSICIANSHIP

Come Raggio Di Sol, *Caldara*

This song must be sung in an extremely sustained, *legato* style. In previous lessons, you have been cautioned not to "scoop" or "slide." True Italian style, however, not only permits this type of connection, but demands it. To visualize the musical line being recommended, imagine the sound that would emanate when a fine violinist slides his finger on the finger board in order to connect two tones of different pitch. In much the same manner, the voice slides from one tone to another. Listen to recordings of fine singers singing Italian art songs or opera. The style will immediately become apparent. To help in your initial attempts, dotted lines have been placed between notes in the song. Where these lines appear, glide the voice from one pitch to the next.

Timing in attack and *duration* of syllables and words are important considerations for "singing in tempo." To sing in tempo, in correct time, requires two basic techniques:

1. Vowels must begin at exactly the same time as their notes begin.

2. Consonants and unstressed diphthong sounds are articulated before or after the vowels.

The following examples will help to make these techniques clear.

Example 1 is measures 4-7 of the song for this lesson, "Come Raggio Di Sol." Note that only the *vowels* from the training text have been included. Consonants and unstressed diphthong sounds have been omitted. Sing this example with vowels only making certain each is attacked at exactly the time the note above it should begin.

In example 2, the consonants and unstressed diphthong sounds have been added so that they occur *before, after,* and *between* the notes. Sing this example making certain that the *vowels* are articulated at exactly the same time as they were in example 1. All syllables and words should now flow in tempo.

These techniques are important considerations for singers. Instrumentalists do not have these problems. They activate a reed, string, or column of air and produce sound almost instantly. The singer of English, a language containing thirteen vowels, six diphthongs, and six kinds of consonants in many combinations, must master the attack and proper duration of all sounds. Otherwise, notes will appear late, particularly when singing with instrumental accompaniment or in a chorus. Even professional soloists must be reminded of these principles.

Review all the songs you have learned, making certain that you "vowel in tempo."

Memorize the following:

Affrett (affrettando): hurrying, quickening accelerating the time
Tranquillo: in a tranquil, restful manner
Stent (stentato): hard, forced, loud, labored
dim assai (diminuendo assai): much softer
simile: in like manner
ppp (pianissimo): as soft as possible
col canto: with the melody

Measure 4: Do not sing in a static, "beaty" fashion. A group of repeated notes usually leads to a climax note and is sung with a slight *crescendo.* Have a feeling of singing "through" this measure as well as measures 8-9, 12-13, 16-17, 22-23, 25-26, 36-37, and 39-40.

Measure 16: In addition to accelerating the speed slightly, intensify the vocal sound and color the voice with a feeling of agitation. Do not employ much volume before measures 23-27.

Measure 28: Make a contrast of mood to one of serenity and calm.

Measure 36: Observe the stress markings (—), singing with a slightly weighted, heavier tone.

Note to the accompanist: The piano accompaniment is to be played *semi legato* (⌒·····) throughout.

Along with "Come Raggio Di Sol," study on page 218 César Franck's famous sacred song "O Lord Most Holy." This song requires a broad, "spun-out" vocal line. Sing with reverence and emotion. Make the vocal line "fit" the tempo of the underlying eighth notes in the accompaniment.

Caldara was a contemporary of the two great Baroque masters, Handel and Bach, and his music reflects the same traditions. Although a Viennese musician, he was Italian both in origin and schooling. He composed 87 operas, 36 oratorios, and much fine church and instrumental music. He had a deep love of euphony and expressiveness, which resulted in a lovely, flowing, melodic style. "Come Raggio Di Sol" is perhaps his most famous song.

COME RAGGIO DI SOL
As from the Shining Sun

Antonio Caldara
(1670—1736)

Sostenuto

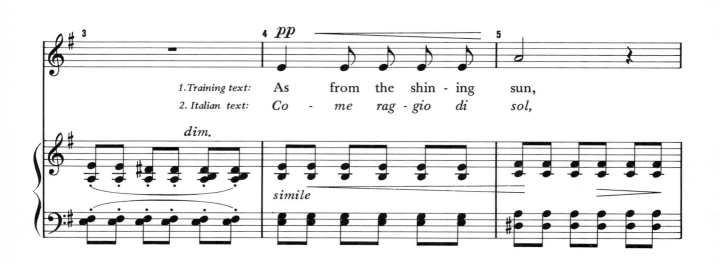

1. Training text: As from the shin - ing sun,
2. Italian text: Co - me rag - gio di sol,

soft - ly re - flec - ted, as from the shin - ing
mi - te e se - re - no, co - me rag - gio di

15

Consonants Articulated
with the Tip of the Tongue

Webster: th, t, d, n, l
International: θ, ð, t, d, n, l

WORDS WITH THE TIP-OF-TONGUE CONSONANTS

Read aloud slowly:

throw	taught	do	new	leap
thing	two	die	none	late
them	shut	done	not	shall
the	fit	and	need	will

Sing.

throw ___ taught ___ do ___ new ___ leap ___ thing ___ two ___ die

none— late— them— shut— done— not— shall— and

3.

thing— throw— them— two— fit— taught— die— do

none— new— need— not— late— leap— will— shall

4.

thing— throw— two— fit— die— do— none— new
late— leap— them— the— taught— and— need— will

SENTENCES WITH THE TIP-OF-TONGUE CONSONANTS

Sing until all consonants are clearly executed.

1.

(a) Think ____ through ____ these ____ truths.
(b) Tom ____ bought ____ two ____ tents.
(c) Dead ____ dogs ____ don't ____ dig.
(d) Ned ____ crooned ____ "New ____ Moon."
(e) Nell ____ will ____ leave ____ late.

2.

(a) Think ____ through ____ these ____ truths. ____
(b) Tom ____ bought ____ two ____ tents. ____
(c) Dead ____ dogs ____ don't ____ dig. ____
(d) Ned ____ crooned ____ "New ____ Moon." ____
(e) Nell ____ will ____ leave ____ late. ____

141

a) Think _____ through ___ these _____ truths. _ b) Tom _____ bought ___ two _____ tents. _____
c) Dead _____ dogs _____ don't _____ dig. __ d) Ned _____ crooned __ "New _____ Moon." ___
e) Nell _____ will _____ leave _____ late. __ f) Shall _____ they _____ shut _____ down? ____

a) Think _____ through _____ these _____ truths.
b) Tom _____ bought _____ two _____ tents.
c) Dead _____ dogs _____ don't _____ dig.
d) Ned _____ crooned _____ "New _____ Moon."
e) Nell _____ will _____ leave _____ late.

STUDY

The Tip-of-Tongue Consonants (th, t, d, n, l): Description and Execution

Th (th) is a continuant and may be voiced or voiceless. It is sung as follows:

1. The tip of the tongue is placed lightly against the edge of the upper front teeth.
2. When *th* is voiced, the *voice* is emitted over the tongue.
3. When *th* is voiceless, the *breath* is emitted over the tongue.

Th is voiced in the following:

this   rather   that   brother   the   bother   with*   mother

Th is voiceless in the following:

thing   thank   throw   thin   tenth   twelfth   author   Keith

When *th* is voiceless, it is a sibilant.

T (t) is voiceless and is stop-plosive. Articulate *t* as follows:

1. Place the tip of the tongue lightly against the gums of the upper front teeth.
2. Drop the tongue quickly, and at the same time emit a puff of breath over it.

D (d) is voiced and is stop-plosive. Sing *d* as follows:

1. The tip of the tongue is flattened against the gums of the upper front teeth.
2. Drop the tongue quickly, and at the same time emit the voice over it.

* Optionally voiced in speech, but always in singing.

142

N(n) is a voiced, nasal continuant, and is sung as follows:

1. The tip of the tongue is flattened against the gums of the upper front teeth.
2. While this position is held, the voice is emitted through the nose.

L(l) is voiced and is a continuant. Sing *l* as follows:

1. The tip of the tongue is placed lightly against the gum of the upper front teeth.
2. The front of the tongue is spread widely against the hard palate.
3. While this position is held, the voice is emitted over the sides of the tongue.

The Tip-of-Tongue Consonants (θ, ð, t, d, n, l): Common Faults and Corrections

Th: use only the tip of the tongue, avoiding tightness and rigidity at the base. Move the tongue quickly, or a thick, guttural sound will result.

In voiceless *th,* exaggerate slightly the hiss of breath, or the word will not be understood. Without the hiss, one would sing *ink* for *think, burr* for *birth,* and *wrong* for *throng.*

In voiced *th,* exaggerate the vocalized sound; without this sound, one sings *eye* for *thy,* and *us* for *thus.*

An extraneous vowel should not sound when *th* follows *n* or *l* (*on - uh these, all - uh things*). To avoid this, use the same tongue position for *n* and *l* as for *th.* For example, when singing *on these,* allow the tip of the tongue to extend outside the edge of the upper front teeth: *n, l,* and *th* can be articulated from this position. The tongue does not have to be moved twice.

Caution: For *l,* even though the same position is used, the tongue tip must move back at the instant *th* is sounded.

The tongue position described above should be used when *th,* followed by *s* (pronounced *z*), appears at the end of the word; *th* is not omitted. Sing *truths,* not *trues,* and *mouths,* not *mouze.*

When *th* occurs before a syllable or a vowel sound, it should be connected with that syllable or vowel sound. Sing *mo - ther,* not *moth - er,* and *no - thing,* not *noth - ing.*

When voiceless *th* is followed by a consonant or a stop, do not add an extraneous vowel sound (*death - uh with, my last breath - uh*). Exaggerate the puff of breath, keeping the tongue in position until the breath is stopped. Observe the same rule for voiced *th* before a consonant or a stop.

T: this consonant is often omitted, or sung inaudibly. To articulate *t,* the tongue tip should be activated where the upper gum ridge curves into the hard palate. Do not flatten the tongue or allow it to touch the teeth. Make the puff of breath accompanying *t* audible; otherwise *d* will be sounded. Do not sing *bedder* for *better,* or *sidder* for *sitter.* Tongue action is rapid, darting away from the upper gum ridge at the moment of aspiration. *Do not omit* t *at the ends of words.* Sing *guest,* not *guess, wait,* not *weigh,* and *blessed** not *bless.* Exaggerate *t* when practicing these words.

When *t* occurs before a vowel or syllable, it is attached to that vowel or syllable. For example, sing *be - tter,* not *bett - er,* and *i -tis,* not *it is.* Exaggerate the puff of breath accompanying *t* before a consonant or a stop (*waiT for me, she is sweeT*), but do not allow another vowel to sound (*wait - uh for me, she is*

* Note that *-ed* is pronounced *t* when it occurs after a voiceless consonant in one-syllable words.

sweet - uh). Articulate *t* a split second before the consonant. Do not allow vocalized sound to accompany *t* before the stop.

When *t* occurs at the beginning of a final syllable, it must be clearly articulated. Sing *li - ttle*, not *lill*, and *bea - ten*, not *bean*.

D: d is a voiced consonant. With two exceptions, discussed below, *d* and *t* are similarly articulated. Do not confuse the two: *d* requires voice, *t* requires breath.

D is treated exactly like *b* (lesson 13) before a stop or consonant. That is, the vowel *uh* must accompany *d*. Without *uh,* there is no *d*.

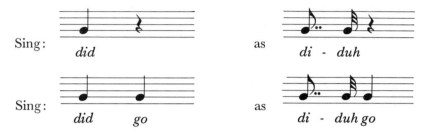

Many words in English end with *d*. Unless the technique described above is mastered, these words will not be understood.

Caution: When *d* ends a word preceding another word beginning with *d*, the *uh* sound is unnecessary, since only one *d* is sounded. Sing *and die* as *an - die,* not *and - uh die*.

N: the rules for singing *n* are much the same as those for singing *m* (lesson 13). Prolong *n* whenever possible. Sing *n* between vowels on the pitch of the first vowel only, or you will scoop. Avoid an *uh* sound when *n* precedes a consonant (*Drink to me on - uh ly*). When *n* occurs at the end of a word, keep the tongue in position until the tone is stopped.

L: when *l* occurs before or between vowel sounds, it is connected to the vowel sound that it precedes. Sing *lu -lla - by*, not *lull - a - by*, and *me-lo - dy*, not *mel - o - dy*. Do not prolong *l* when it precedes a vowel or appears between vowels. This causes a throaty tone and tends to muddle the diction. Articulate *l* quickly by a flip of the tongue.

When *l* occurs after a vowel, it *should* be prolonged, and the tongue should *not* be flipped. Without a prolonged *l*, the sense of many words will be lost. If the tongue is flipped, an unnecessary *uh* will be heard. Sing *yell*, not *yea* or *yell - uh*, *isle,* not *I* or *isle - uh,* and *wills*, not *wiz* or *wills - uh*. Keep the tongue in position for *l* until the tone is stopped.

Take care to execute *l* clearly when it precedes *d*. Do not sing *mode* for *mold*, and *rode* for *rolled*.

It has been observed that *l* is sometimes silent. Do not sing *l* in words such as *talk, walk, psalm, folk,* and *half*.

Do not diphthongize pure vowels that precede *l*. Avoid singing *dee -uhl* for *deal* and *roo - uhl* for *rule*. Move the tongue into position for *l* at the instant that *l* is sounded.

SONG INTERPRETATION AND MUSICIANSHIP

The Night, *Richard Strauss*

This is a dramatic mood piece calling for a sensitive relationship between the melody and the accompaniment.

144

Memorize the following:

Sotto voce: softly; in an undertone
Una corda: use the soft pedal on the piano
Measures 2-17: Sing without using the full voice. Use a *mezzo voce* production. Allow the vocal line to blend with the accompaniment.

Measures 15 and 24: Sing delicately. A light, almost breathy quality will provide the best coloring.

Measures 18-24: Add more movement and a brighter tone. Distinguish between ♪ ♪ and ♪. ♪

Measures 28–30: Add more weight to the tone. The feeling, however, is one of breadth rather than of loudness.

Measures 34-40: Note that the climax is reached at *pp*.

Measures 41-45: This is the postlude. Do not break the mood until the piano concludes.

A complete contrast to the dramatic intensity of "The Night" is DePue's "Lullaby" on page 223. Sing this song very simply and quite softly. For another "Lullaby," study the famous one by Brahms.

Richard Strauss was one of the greatest figures in music during the last decade of the nineteenth century. He was a prominent composer, a master orchestrator, and an expert conductor. He developed the symphonic poem to its highest form, wrote highly successful operas and many beautiful songs. "The Night" is from Opus 10, Acht Gedichte (eight poems), one of his earlier compositions.

THE NIGHT
Die Nacht

Herrmann von Gilm

Richard Strauss
(1864 - 1949)

1. Training text: Comes the night _____ o'er hill and dell,
2. German text: Aus dem Wal - de tritt die Nacht,

Dark-'ning woods that once were light-ed; Now, be-hold, the
aus dem Bäu-men schleicht sie lei-se, schaut sich um in

day has end-ed, dark-ness reigns!
wei-tem Krei-se, nun gib Acht.

we would hold, cov - ers sil -ver from the stream,
was nur hold, *nimmt das Sil - ber weg des Stroms,*

cov - ers can -dle's light a - gleam, all the gold!
nimmt von Kup - fer - dach des Doms *weg das Gold.*

Ped. ✳

p

dim.

Ped. ✳ Ped. ✳

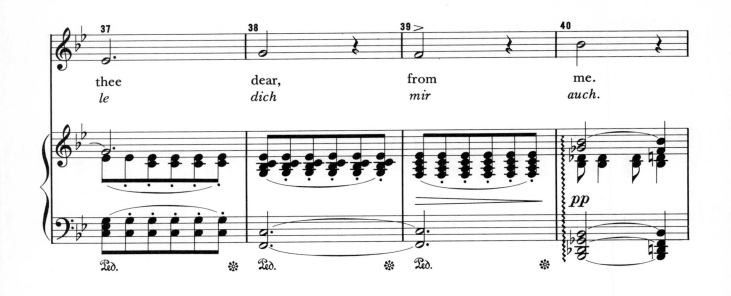

thee   dear,   from   me.
le   *dich*   *mir*   *auch.*

16

Consonants Articulated
with the Tongue and Gum

Webster: s, z, sh, zh, r
International: s, z, ʃ, ʒ, r

WORDS WITH THE TONGUE AND GUM CONSONANTS

Read aloud slowly:

sing	zest	show	azure	run
pass	zeal	push	vision	breath
see	poise	hush	pleasure	cry
so	choose	short	leisure	far

Sing.

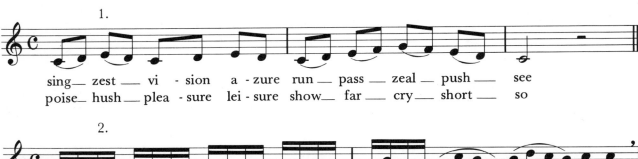

run ___ breath ___ cry ___ push ___ show ___ hush ___ poise ___ lei - sure

3.

sing ___ pass ___ see ___ zest ___ zeal ___ poise ___ show ___ push

hush³ ___ a ³ - zure ___ vi - sion ___ run ___ cry ___ far

4.

so ___ choose ___ short ___ lei - sure ___ far ___ sing ___ zest ___ a - zure
show ___ run ___ pass ___ vi - sion ___ zeal ___ push ___ breath plea - sure

SENTENCES WITH THE TONGUE AND GUM CONSONANTS

Sing until all consonants are clearly executed.

1.

(a) Sis ___ sings ___ sweet ___ songs. ___
(b) Please ___ choose ___ his ___ clothes. ___
(c) Lei - sure ___ some - times ___ mea - sures ___ plea - sure. ___
(d) Shops ___ show ___ fresh ___ fish. ___
(e) Girls ___ wear ___ red ___ rouge. ___

2.

(a) Sis ___ sings ___ sweet ___ songs. ___
(b) Please ___ choose ___ his ___ clothes. ___
(c) Shops ___ show ___ fresh ___ fish. ___
(d) Lei - sure ___ some - times ___ mea - sures ___ plea - sure. ___
(e) Girls ___ wear ___ red ___ rouge. ___

153

3.

(a) Sis —— sings —— sweet —— songs. (b) Please —— choose —— his —— clothes. ——
(c) Shops —— show —— fresh —— fish. — (d) Lei - sure — some-times — mea - sures — plea - sure.
(e) Girls —— wear —— red —— rouge. (f) She —— has —— a - zure eyes. ——

4.

(a) Sis ———— sings ———— sweet ———— songs. ————
(b) Please ———— choose ———— his ———— clothes. ————
(c) Shops ———— show ———— fresh ———— fish. ————
(d) Lei - sure some - times mea - sures plea - sure.
(e) Girls ———— wear ———— red ———— rouge. ————

STUDY

The Tongue and Gum Consonants (s, z, sh, zh, r): Description and Execution

The consonant s(s), sometimes spelled c, is a voiceless continuant. Sing s as follows:

1. The tip of the tongue is raised toward, but does not touch, the center of the upper front teeth.
2. The sides of the tongue are against the upper side teeth.
3. While this position is held, the breath is emitted over the groove of the tongue and between the nearly closed front teeth.

S is a sibilant.

Z(z), sometimes spelled $s,$ is a voiced continuant, and is sung as follows:

1. The tip of the tongue is raised toward, but does not touch, the center of the upper front teeth.
2. The sides of the tongue are against the upper side teeth.
3. While this position is held, the voice is emitted over the groove of the tongue and between the nearly closed front teeth.

S and z differ only in that s is voiceless and z is voiced.

Sh(sh) is a voiceless continuant and is articulated as follows:

1. The tip of the tongue is raised slightly higher than for $s,$ toward the center of the upper front teeth.
2. The sides of the tongue are placed against the edges of the upper side teeth.
3. While this position is held, the breath is emitted forcefully over the tongue and between nearly closed front teeth.

Sh is a sibilant.

Zh(zh) is a voiced continuant and is sung as follows:

154

1. The tip of the tongue is raised slightly higher than for *s*, toward the center of the upper front teeth.
2. The sides of the tongue are placed against the edges of the upper side teeth.
3. While this position is held, the voice is emitted over the tongue and between nearly closed front teeth.

Sh and *zh* differ only in that *sh* is voiceless and *zh* is voiced.

R(r) may be a voiced continuant, or it may be tongued. As a voiced continuant, *r* is sung as follows:

1. The tip of the tongue is pointed toward the back of the upper front gums.
2. The back of the tongue is down.
3. While this position is held, the voice is emitted over the tongue.

Execute tongued *r* as follows:

1. The tip of the tongue darts against the upper front gums, touching only once.
2. The back of the tongue is down.

In the United States, *r* is commonly used as a voiced continuant. Tongued *r* is commonly used in England.

The Tongue and Gum Consonants (s, z,ʃ, ʒ, r): Common Faults and Corrections

S and *z:* these consonants do not usually present problems except to those who lisp. Lispers should study the section describing these sounds and their execution. Lisping is usually caused by incorrect tongue or lip position. The tip of the tongue must be in the center of the mouth, close to the upper teeth, but not touching. Do not place the tongue tip against the lower gum or teeth. Hold the sides of the tongue against the upper side teeth, or breath will escape laterally. Do not attempt too forceful an emission of breath. Keep the lips in an oval, relaxed position. Check with a hand mirror to avoid a crooked lip position.

When *s* or *z* is followed by a syllable or a word beginning with a vowel, it is attached to that syllable or vowel. Sing *pa - ssing by,* not *pass - ing by,* and *ri - zup,* not *rise up.*

When *s* or *z* is followed by a consonant or a stop, do not add *uh.* Sing *ki - ssme,* not *kiss-uh me, choo - zyour,* not *choose - uh your,* and *He arose,* not *He arose - uh.* Do not move the tongue until the breath or tone stops.

When *s* ends a word before a word beginning with *s,* only one prolonged *s* is sounded. *Let us see* is sung, *Le - tu - see.* The same rule applies to *z.*

When *s...z* or *z...s* occur together, do not try to separate them. Merge the two sounds (*His zeal*).

Sh(ʃ) and *zh*(ʒ): make certain that *sh* is aspirated and *zh* is voiced. When either is followed by a syllable, or a word beginning with a vowel, it is attached to that syllable or vowel. Sing *pu - shing,* not *push - ing,* and *vi - sion,* not *vis - ion.*

Do not allow an *uh* to sound when *sh* or *zh* precedes a consonant or a stop. Sing *hu - shnow,* not *hush - uh now,* and *prestige,* not *prestige - uh.*

When *sh* precedes another *sh* (*And all flesh shall see it together*), merge the two into one prolonged *sh.*

R: soften r before a consonant sound or stop. If a clear voiced *r* is sung, the vowel preceding *r* will be distorted by the movement of the tongue upwards.

If tongued *r* is sung, diction sounds affected and artificial.

In the following words, notice that when *r* is softened before a consonant or stop, a diphthong is sounded:

lord	is sung	*law⌢uh(r)d*
arm	is sung	*ah⌢uh(r)m*
morning	is sung	*maw⌢uh(r)ning*
for you	is sung	*faw⌢uh(r) you*
near me	is sung	*nih⌢uh(r) me*
their love	is sung	*theh⌢uh(r) love*
never	is sung	*neh⌢vuh(r)*

To achieve clarity on extremely high tones, even before a consonant or stop, sing tongued *r*.

The vowel preceding a softened *r* is prolonged for its full value and is pure. *Park* is sung *pah - uh(r)k,* not *pock; mark* is *mah - uh(r)k,* not *mock.* When *r* ends a word before another word beginning with *r,* the first *r* is omitted and the second sounded as a voiced continuant.

Always sing r *before a vowel sound* and attach it to that vowel sound:

a - round	not	*ar - ound*
bo - row*	not	*bor - row*
spi - rit	not	*spir - it*
fo - rall	not	*for all*

Sing tongued *r* in opera and between vowel sounds in sacred and art songs. At other times, sing voiced *r.*

When *r* follows *t* or *d* (*train, trip, drain, drip*), even though in opera, art, or sacred song, it is voiced.

When *cr* or *gr* combinations occur in dramatic or color words (*cry, cruel, grief, great*) use tongued *r.*

Never use tongued *r* in popular songs, American folk songs, musical comedy (excepting Gilbert and Sullivan) or patriotic songs, for tongued *r* sounds affected and pretentious.

Avoid "burring" in voiced *r.* Keep the back of the tongue down, away from the palate, or a guttural, flat, burred sound results.

SONG INTERPRETATION AND MUSICIANSHIP

Because, *D'Hardelot*

A favorite since it was composed, "Because" continues to be a popular solo for weddings. The romantic, sentimental quality of the work permits more freedom of interpretation than is usual in songs of the classical or even the romantic period. Some liberties of tempo and dynamics are allowable, but they should not be excessive.

Measure 9: Clap the rhythm ♩. ♪ ♪. ♪ ♪ ♪ ♪ ♪ and speak the words in this rhythm before singing. This pattern occurs several times (measures 15, 17, 19, 30). After the basic rhythm is mastered in strict tempo, sing, using the *rubato* style. Each time the measure is repeated, stress a different word or note. Keep the underlying beat steady.

Measure 15: Do not "bounce" the ♪ ♪ ♪ ♪ notes. Keep them as connected as possible.

Measures 17-19: These are sequences of measure 15. Each succeeding group is to be performed more loudly and intensely.

* Sound only one *r* in *rr.*

156

Measure 19: Sing with *rubato.*

Measures 21-24: If the long high note cannot be sustained, breathe after the word *because* in measure 21.

Measure 25: Sing broadly with full resonance.

Two more songs are recommended for study at the back of the book. The first (on p. 226) is "Silent Noon" by Ralph Vaughan Williams. This song contrasts sharply in style with "The Vagabond." It requires excellent control of breath and tone. Vocal lines are long with many dynamic changes. Sing this song first on a neutral syllable, then with text. Be careful not to force the voice. Seek to exercise complete control of the breath with firm support for every tone.

The second song, "Down Among the Dead Men" (page 231), is a robust one for male voice. This old English "drinking song" should be sung with abandon and full voice. In the last six bars, control the crescendo so that the climax is reached in the last bar. Do not be tempted to "yell" this song. Sing at dynamic levels that you can control without forcing.

BECAUSE

English words by
Edward Teschemacher

Guy d'Hardelot
(1858—1936)

Be - cause ———— you come to me ———— with naught save
Lors - que j'en -tends ton pas, ——— comme en un

love, ——— And hold my hand and lift mine eyes a - bove, ——— A
rê - ve Le fol es - poir de te re - voir s'é - lè - ve, Et

159

Be - cause ——— God made thee
Et puis ——— tu viens à

mine, ——————— I'll cher - ish thee ——————— Through
moi ——————— et je fris - son - ne, *Tu*

light and dark - ness, through all time to be, ——— And
prends ma main, et tout mon coeur se don - ne A

17

Consonants Articulated with the Tongue and Hard Palate

Webster: y, ch, j
International: j, tʃ, dʒ

WORDS WITH THE TONGUE AND HARD PALATE CONSONANTS

Read aloud slowly:

yes	charm	June
yet	chance	just
yield	such	age
yearn	choose	ridge

Sing.

1.

yes — charm — June — yet — chance — just — yield — such — age.
yearn — choose — ridge — such — charm — June — age — yet — yes.

2.

choose — such — chance — charm — ridge — age — just — June

yearn ____ yield ____ yet ____ yes ____ chance ____ age ____ such ____ yet.

3.

yes ____ yet ____ yield ____ yearn ____ charm ____ chance ____ such ____ choose

June ____ just ____ age ____ ridge ____ yawn ____ yore ____ cheer ____ jaw

4.

yes ____ yet ____ yield ____ yearn ____ charm ____ chance ____ such ____ choose
June ____ just ____ age ____ ridge ____ youth ____ chaste ____ jaw ____ chin

SENTENCES WITH THE TONGUE AND HARD PALATE CONSONANTS

Sing until all consonants are clearly executed:

1.

(a) You ____ use ____ your ____ yacht.
(b) Chimes ____ charm ____ church ____ es.
(c) John's ____ grudge ____ jolts ____ Jim.
(d) Age ____ chides ____ youth's ____ cheer.

2.

(a) You ____ use ____ your ____ yacht. ____
(b) Chimes ____ charm ____ church ____ es. ____
(c) John's ____ grudge ____ jolts ____ Jim. ____
(d) Age ____ chides ____ youth's ____ cheer. ____

165

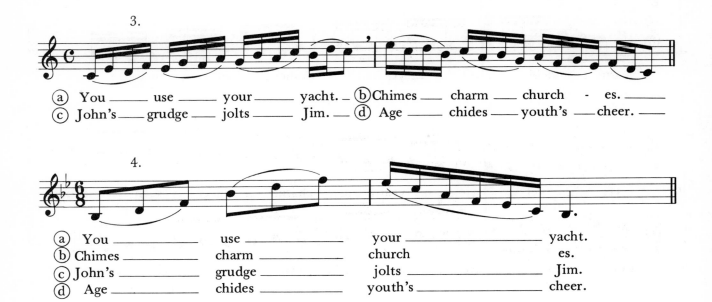

3.

(a) You ——— use ——— your ——— yacht. — (b) Chimes —— charm —— church - es. ———
(c) John's —— grudge —— jolts ——— Jim. — (d) Age ——— chides —— youth's —— cheer. ——

4.

(a) You ——————— use ——————— your ——————— yacht.
(b) Chimes ————— charm ————— church es.
(c) John's ————— grudge ————— jolts ————— Jim.
(d) Age ————— chides ————— youth's ————— cheer.

STUDY

The Tongue and Hard Palate Consonants (y, ch, j): Description and Execution

Y(y) is a voiced continuant and is articulated as follows:

1. The tip of the tongue is forward.
2. The middle of the tongue is raised toward the hard palate, with the sides of the tongue against the upper side teeth.
3. The voice is emitted over the tongue.

Ch(ch) is two voiceless consonants blended together and should be executed as follows:

1. The consonant *t* is articulated with the plosive omitted.
2. The tip of the tongue glides back from the gums over the front of the hard palate and drops quickly as the sibilant *sh* is emitted over it.

Remember that *t* is plosive and *sh* continuant. The two consonants must be blended together by a rapid movement of the tongue, so that *ch* will be clear and distinct.

J(j), sometimes spelled *g*, is a blend of two voiced consonants. Execute *j* as follows:

1. The consonant *d* is articulated with the plosive omitted.
2. The tip of the tongue glides back from the gums over the front of the hard palate and drops quickly as voiced *zh* is emitted over it.

Remember that *d* is plosive and *zh* continuant. Blend the two together smoothly and clearly.

Ch and *j* are called *blended consonants,* the only ones in English. All other consonants have single, unique sounds. *Ch* and *j* are, to consonants, what diphthongs are to vowels.

166

The Tongue and Hard Palate Consonants (j, tʃ, dʒ): Common Faults and Corrections

Y (j): y is sometimes a vowel sound. Memorize the following rules in order to recognize *y* as a consonant or vowel.

1. At the beginning of a syllable, *y* is a consonant.

young	*lawyer*
yield	*barnyard*

2. At all other times, *y* is a vowel.

carry	*marry*
merry	*rhythm*

When *y* occurs unstressed at the end of a word, it has the *IH* sound (*marry, merry*).

Caution: When words like *marry* and *merry* are rhymed with *EE* words (*me, be, she*), *y* still has the *IH* sound.

When *y* follows a word ending with a consonant, the consonant is attached to *y* (*lo -vyou*, not *love - uh you*, and *leapyear*, not *leap - uh year*). Be particularly careful of the word *you* when it is preceded by a word ending with a consonant:

want you	is	*wan - tyou*	not	*one - chew*
did you	is	*did - uh you*	not	*di - djew*
bless you	is	*ble - syou*	not	*ble - shew*

Ch and *j* (tʃ, dʒ): *ch* must be voiceless; *j* is voiced. Do not sing *chon* for *John*, *chust* for *just*, or *chest* for *jest*.

When *ch* or *j* occurs before a syllable or a word beginning with a vowel sound, it is attached to that syllable or vowel (*su - chis* for *such is*, and *pa - jate* for *page eight*).

When *ch* or *j* occurs before a consonant sound or a stop, avoid an extra *uh* sound (*tea - chme*, not *teach - uh me*, and *a - gto age*, not *age - uh to age - uh*).

When *ch* ends a word preceding another word beginning with *ch*, each *ch* must be sounded. The same rule applies to *j* (*such cheer* as *such/cheer*, not *su - cheer* or *such - uh cheer*, and *Judge James* as *Judge/James*, not *Juh -James*, or *Judge - uh James*).

SONG INTERPRETATION AND MUSICIANSHIP

When I Was A Lad, *Sullivan*

This delightful "patter song" from *H.M.S. Pinafore*, one of Gilbert and Sullivan's most popular operettas, is a tongue twister. To articulate these words clearly requires painstaking work on all the principles of English diction.

Sir Joseph Porter, the pompous, stuffy First Lord of the Admiralty, outlines the history of his rise to power and tells his listeners on board the good ship H.M.S. "Pinafore" how they can all "be rulers of the Queen's Navee." This song is an ideal *staccato* study and should be practiced on all vowels, with each note articulated separately.

Use this song as an articulation study by making up neutral syllables involving consonants. Place these consonants before vowels (*TAH*), after vowels (*AT*), or before and after vowels (*TAHT*). Practice slowly at first and then accelerate.

The small-sized (cue) notes (measure 7) indicate that in some verse other than verse 1 there is another syllable or word that must be included within the beat.

When using the words of the text, practice speaking in rhythm but without music until the text is clear. Then add music.

Although this is a song for a male voice, girls should sing it also for diction practice. Girls may substitute *lass* for *lad*, and *girl* for *boy*.

The word *clerk* in this song should be given the British pronunciation *clark*.

Other Gilbert and Sullivan patter songs you may wish to learn are:

"I am the Very Model,"	*Pirates of Penzance*
"I've Got a Little List,"	*The Mikado*
"Said I to Myself,"	*Iolanthe*
"I Stole a Prince,"	*Gondoliers*
"There Lived a King,"	*Gondoliers*
"When I, Good Friends, Was Called to the Bar,"	*Trial By Jury*
"A Private Buffoon,"	*Yeoman of the Guard*

Study also two more songs at the back of the book: Carl Engel's "Sea-Shell" (page 233) and Reynaldo Hahn's "The Hour of Dreaming" (page 236).

Carl Engel was born in Germany in 1818 and died in England in 1882. He is remembered not only as a composer but also as an eminent writer about musical instruments. Because the *tessitura* of "Sea-Shell" is fairly high, low voices may find the song more comfortable in the key of E-flat. Sing with simplicity at the beginning, then follow the composer's instructions. A new term in this song is *ravvivando*, which means "quickening."

Reynaldo Hahn, though born in Caracas, Venezuela, in 1874, received his musical education in Paris. He wrote many kinds of music but is remembered primarily for his songs. "The Hour of Dreaming" ("L'Heure exquise") is a mood piece typical of French music written in the early part of the twentieth century. The voice and the piano, acting as partners, should seek to "paint a picture." Note that all three high F's are sung softly. Lower male voices will probably wish to sing these pitches *falsetto*. Some may wish to transpose the key down to B-flat.

Sir Joseph outlines his rise to power and tells how all can be "rulers of the Queen's Navee."

WHEN I WAS A LAD

Sir William S. Gilbert

Sir Arthur S. Sullivan
(1842–1900)

Sir Joseph

171

18

Consonants Articulated
with the Back of the Tongue

Webster: k, g, ng
International: k, g, ŋ

WORDS WITH THE BACK-OF-TONGUE CONSONANTS

Read aloud slowly:

king	God	sing
kind	give	long
kick	grieve	bring
come	big	sung

Sing.

1.

king — God — sing — kind — give — long — kick — grieve — bring.
come — big — sung — king — kind — God — give — sing — long.

2.

king — kind — kick — come — God — give — grieve — big

sing —— long —— bring —— sung —— big —— grieve —— give —— God.

3.

king —— kind —— kick —— come —— God —— give —— grieve —— big

sing —— long —— bring —— sung —— queen —— grip —— ring —— cake.

4.

king —— king —— kick —— come —— God —— give —— grieve —— big.
sing —— long —— bring —— sung —— queen —— egg —— green —— wrong.

SENTENCES WITH THE BACK-OF-TONGUE CONSONANTS

Sing until all consonants are clearly excuted:

1.

ⓐ Kings ——————— can ——————— crown ——————— counts.
ⓑ Big ——————— bugs ——————— bring ——————— grief.
ⓒ Sing ——————— songs; ——————— ring ——————— gongs.
ⓓ Kind ——————— goats ——————— don't ——————— kick.

2.

ⓐ Kings ——————— can ——————— crown ——————— counts. ———————
ⓑ Big ——————— bugs ——————— bring ——————— grief. ———————
ⓒ Sing ——————— songs; ——————— ring ——————— gongs. ———————
ⓓ Kind ——————— goats ——————— don't ——————— kick. ———————

STUDY

The Back-of-Tongue Consonants (k, g, ng): Description and Execution

K(k) sometimes spelled *c*, *ck*, *q*, and *ch* is voiceless and stop-plosive. Articulate *k* as follows:

1. The tip of the tongue is forward.
2. The back of the tongue is raised against the soft palate.
3. The tongue is quickly lowered; breath is emitted over the tongue plosively.

G(g) is a voiced stop-plosive and is articulated as follows:

1. The tip of the tongue is forward.
2. The back of the tongue is raised against the soft palate.
3. The tongue is lowered quickly; the voice is emitted over the tongue plosively.

Ng(ng) is a voiced, nasal continuant and should be articulated as follows:

1. The tip of the tongue is forward.
2. The back of the tongue is raised against the soft palate.
3. While this position is held, the voice is emitted through the nose.

The Back-of-Tongue Consonants (k, g, ŋ): Common Faults and Corrections

K and *g:* many singers produce *h* rather than *k* because they do not make contact between the tongue and soft palate. Some singers voice the consonant, singing *g* rather than *k*. The reason for these mistakes is more psychological than physical. Singers are fearful of plosive, crisp sounds, particularly when singing *pp* or *legato.* Crisply articulated *k's* and hard *g's* add to expressive singing.

K or *g* before a syllable, or a word beginning with a vowel, is attached to the syllable or vowel (*wal - king* for *walking,* and *tri - gger* for *trigger.*

K before a consonant is articulated just before the consonant. Do not add an *uh* sound (*dar - kwater,* not *dark - uh water*).

176

K before *t* or *ts* must not be omitted. To avoid this fault, practice the following:

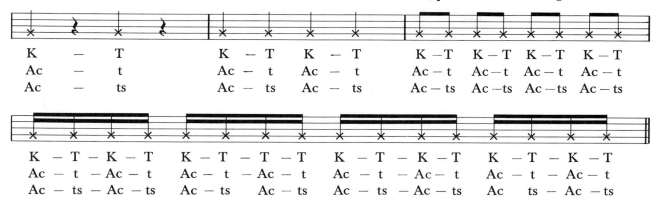

K	—	T		K	—	T	K	—	T		K	–T	K	–T	K	–T	K	–T
Ac	—	t		Ac	—	t	Ac	—	t		Ac	–t	Ac	–t	Ac	–t	Ac	–t
Ac	—	ts		Ac	—	ts	Ac	—	ts		Ac	–ts	Ac	–ts	Ac	–ts	Ac	–ts

K	–	T	–	K	–	T		K	–	T	–	T	–	T		K	–	T	–	K	–T		K	–	T	–	K	–T
Ac	–	t	–	Ac	–	t		Ac	–	t	–	Ac	–	t		Ac	–	t	–	Ac–	t		Ac	–	t	–	Ac	– t
Ac	–	ts	–	Ac	–	ts		Ac	–	ts		Ac	–	ts		Ac	–	ts	–	Ac	–ts		Ac		ts	–	Ac	–ts

1. Whisper the sounds slowly.
2. Sing, gradually increasing speed.

When *k* ends a word preceding another word beginning with *k,* stop the first *k* without adding the plosive sound (called *implosion*), and explode the second *k* only (*speak quickly* as *spea | quickly,* not *speak - uh quickly*).

When *g* occurs before a consonant or stop, it is treated exactly as *b* (lesson 13) and *d* (lesson 15) are treated. That is, the weak vowel is appended, or *g* will not sound. Sing:

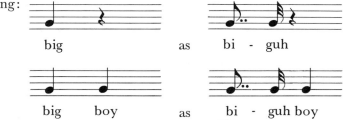

There is one exception to this rule. When *g* (*b, d*) occurs before a word beginning with *w* or *y,* the weak vowel is not sounded and *g* is attached to *w* or *y* (*big year* as *bi - gyear, rob you* as *ro - byou,* and *dead wood* as *dea - dwood*).

SONG INTERPRETATION AND MUSICIANSHIP

Who Is Sylvia?, *Schubert*

Measure 5: Make a slight *crescendo* into measure 6. When singing the ♩., do not slide pitch *A* into pitch *F.*

Measure 6: Make a slight stress on *Syl* with a fast ⟩ on - *via.*

Measures 7–8: Sing as in measures 5 and 6.

Measure 9: Starting with the last note in measure 8, make a long ⟨ to measure 10.

Measure 10: ⟨ slightly on the word *mend,* and ⟩ on the word *her.*

Measure 13: Observe the rest but do not take a breath.

Measures 16–17: Be careful of pitch.

Measure 21: Practice the ♫ figure until each note is on pitch and in correct rhythm.

Measures 23–24: Sing the octaves in tune. Do not stress the upper *C* (measure 23) as much as the upper *D* (measure 24).

Measure 29: Note the :| indicating a repeat from measure 5.

Two final songs have been included for your study. See first John Alden Carpenter's "The Sleep That Flits on Baby's Eyes" (page 240). Carpenter was an American composer born in Chicago in 1876. Composing was more a hobby than a profession, since he was engaged in business most of his life. His music is characterized by delicacy and tender sentiment. This particular song is from the cycle, *Gitanjali,* all the songs from which are set to words by the great Indian poet Rabindranath Tagore.

The other song is "Eldorado," written for this book by Wallace DePue (page 243). Both the piano and voice parts are very difficult and will present a challenge to the most advanced student.

"Eldorado" will introduce a different style of composition from any other song in this book. This style is called "serial" or "twelve-tone row" composition. The songs that you have learned so far have all been in traditional major or minor keys. But "twelve-tone" music has no key! The twelve tones of the chromatic scale are arranged by the composer in any order that he chooses, without repeating any, so that no tone dominates the other eleven. This series of twelve tones, or "row," is then used as the exclusive melodic and harmonic material of the composition. The row may be transposed to begin at any pitch level, may be inverted (turned over), retrograded (used backwards), or combined into chords. The only requirement is that all twelve tones of the row be used before any is repeated. The tones may be given any rhythmic or melodic shape, unless the rhythm itself is serialized.

"Eldorado" is composed so that the row is used in four different ways for each of the four verses of the poem by Edgar Allan Poe:

Verse 1—the original row
Verse 2—inversion of the original row (each interval turned over)
Verse 3—retrograde of the original row (the row sung backwards)
Verse 4—inversion of the retrograde (the row sung backwards but with each
                 interval turned over)

Examples from the song itself should help to make this technique of composition clear. Pitches are placed under the word or syllable with which they occur. Numbers designate where the pitches occur in the row.

Original Row

Verse I: Gayly bedight, a gallant knight, In sunshine and in shadow,

Pitches:	C		G	A♭	E♭		D♭	F	F♯
Numbers:	1		2	3	4		5	6	7

Had journeyed long, Singing a song, In search of Eldorado.

Pitches:	D	B♭		A		B		E
Numbers:	8	9		10		11		12

Inversion of Original Row

Verse 2: But he grew old—This knight so bold,—And o'er his heart a shadow

Pitches:	C		F	E	A		B	G	G♭	B♮
Numbers:	1		2	3	4		5	6	7	8

Fell as he found No spot of ground That looked like Eldorado.

Pitches:	D	E♭	D♭		A♭
Numbers:	9	10	11		12

Retrograde of Original Row

Verse 3: And, as strength Failed him at length, He met a pilgrim shadow,

Pitches:	E	B	A	B♭		D	F♯	F	D♭
Numbers:	12	11	10	9		8	7	6	5

"Shadow," said he, "Where can it be—This place called Eldorado?"

Numbers:	E♭		A♭		G		C
Pitches:	4		3		2		1

Inversion of The Retrograde

Verse 4: "Over the mountains Of the Moon, Down the Valley of the Shadow,

Pitches:	E*	A		B	A♯	F♯	D*	E♭
Numbers:	12	11		10	9	8	7	6

Ride, boldly ride," The shade replied "If you seek for Eldorado!"

Pitches:	G	F*		C	D♭		A♭
Numbers:	5	4		3	2		1

Note that in each row, twelve different pitches are used and no pitch is repeated. Thus no pitch is more important than any other; there is no "key" pitch, no tonal center.

Note that when an interval is inverted, it is simply "turned over." For example:

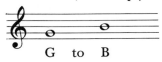

G   to   B

is an interval of a major-third *up*. To invert that interval—to turn it over—we would have to write, from pitch G, an interval of a major third *down:*

G   to   E♭

is an interval of a major-third *down,* the inversion of the first interval. If three intervals are inverted, the following would occur:

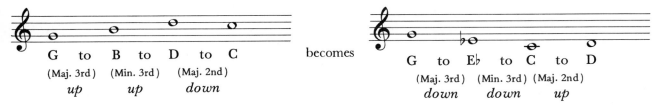

Similarly, all twelve tones of the chromatic scale, arranged in a prescribed order, may be inverted, as was done in verses two and four of "Eldorado." Careful study of the piano part will reveal that it too is made from the rows.**

* Octave displacement. The composer uses the same pitch but at a different octave.
** A few tones have been altered.

To the student seeing and hearing twelve-tone technique for the first time, the system may seem arbitrary and contrived. But it is no more so than the familiar major-minor system. Serial technique does not restrict the imagination of the composer. Rather it frees him from the restriction of keys, thus providing him with a substitute for traditional tonality.

Twelve-tone music is difficult to sing because it lies outside the experience of most students. But there is really no reason a diminished fifth (C to G-flat up), for example, should be more difficult to sing than a major third. We simply must learn to hear such intervals.

Many of the leading composers of the twentieth century have used the twelve-tone system, including Igor Stravinsky, Arnold Schoenberg (who is credited with inventing it), Alban Berg, Anton Webern, Aaron Copland, Gunther Schuller, and Roger Sessions.

Listen to other compositions in this style. Serial compositions might very well constitute much of the music of the future.

The verses for this song are taken from Act IV, scene 2, of Shakespeare's play, Two Gentlemen of Verona. *One of Sylvia's lovers, whose name is Thurio, has written these lyrics and, together with a group of hired musicians, sings them to her.*

WHO IS SYLVIA?

mir - ed ____ be, ____ That she
hab - its ____ there, ____ And be - ing
gar - lands ____ bring, ____ To her

might ad - mir - ed ____ be.
help'd in - hab - its ____ there.
let us gar - lands ____ bring.

To Mlle Nadiejda Rimsky - Korsakov

PASTORALE

Igor Stravinsky
(1882—1971)

MY LOVELY CELIA

George Monro
(b? —d. 1731)

love - ly ___ Ce - lia, heav'n - ly ___ fair, As

li - lies ___ sweet as soft ___ as ___ air; No

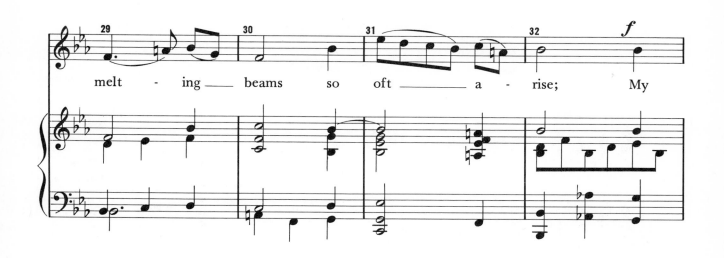

melt - ing — beams so oft — a - rise; My

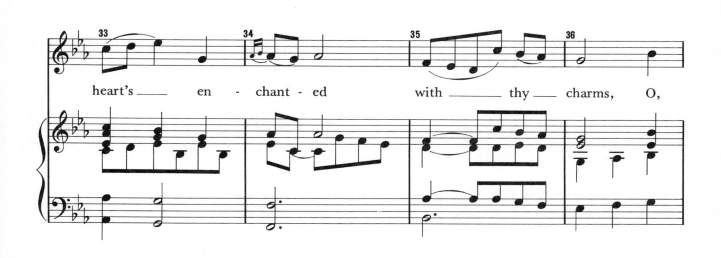

heart's — en - chant - ed with — thy — charms, O,

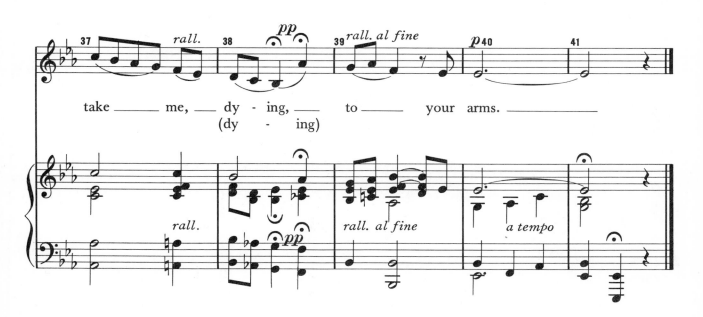

take — me, — dy - ing, — to — your arms. —
(dy - ing)

To Richard and Ethel Mathey

HE'S GONE AWAY

Southern Mountain Song
Arr. by Wallace De Pue

THE SONG OF THE FLEA

From Goethe's *Faust*

Ludwig van Beethoven
(1770—1827)

ev- er a son could__ be   He __ sum-moned forth his tail - or who
cross hang-ing on his __ chest. Then a knight was he ap - point - ed with
wie sei-nen eig'-nen__ Sohn Da rief er sei - nen Schnei - der, der
auch ein Kreuz da - ran, und__ war so-gleich Mi - ni - ster, und

hur - ried to __ the __ throne. "You take my dear friend's meas - ure and
pomp and pag -eant - ry, And all of his re - la - tions were
Schnei-der kam her - an: Da miss dem Jun - ker Klei - der, und
hatt' ei-nen gro - ssen Stern, da wur - den sei - ne Ge - schwi - ster bei

make some clothes for his own!"
al - so made gen - try!
miss ihm Ho - sen - an!
Hof auch gro - sse __ Herr'n.

193

At court, the lords and lad - ies by
Und Herr'n und Frau'n am Ho - fe, die

so many fleas were plagued, the queen and her wait - ing lad - ies were
wa - ren sehr ge - plagt, die Kö - ni - gen und die Zo - fe ge -

bit - ten 'til they aged! They dared not ev - en scratch them, they
sto - chen und ge - nagt, und durf - ten sie nicht kni - cken, und

194

THE LASS WITH THE DELICATE AIR

Thomas Augustine Arne
(1710–1778)

1. Young Mol - ly who — lived at the foot — of — the — hill, Whose fame — ev' - ry — la - dy with en - vy doth fill, Of

2. One eve - ning last — May, as I trav - ersed — the — grove, In thought - less — re - tire - ment, not dream - ing of love, I

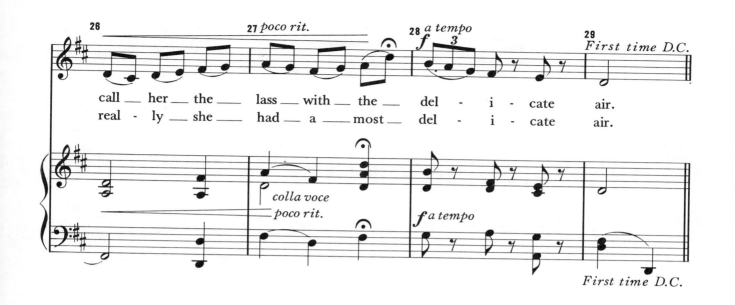

call — her — the — lass — with — the — del - i - cate — air.
real - ly — she — had — a — most — del - i - cate — air.

First time D.C.

3. By a mur - mur - ing — brook, on a green moss - y — knoll, A
4. A — thou - sand times — o'er I've re - peat - ed — my — suit, But

chap - let _ com - pos - ing, the fair _ one with scroll; Sur - prised and _ trans -
still _ the _ tor - men - tor af - fects _ to be mute! Then tell me _ ye _

port - ed _ I _ could not _ for - bear _ With _ rap - ture _ to _
swains who _ have _ con - quered _ the _ fair, _ How to win the _ dear _

gaze on her del - i - cate air, on her del - - - -
lass with the del - i - cate air, with the del - - - -

-i-cate air, With __ rap-ture __ to __ gaze __ on __ her __ del - i -cate __

-i-cate air,__ How to

air.

win __ the __ dear __ lass __ with __ the __ del - i - cate __ air.

201

DIDO'S LAMENT
From Dido and Aeneas (1680?)

Nahum Tate

Henry Purcell
(1658? —1695)

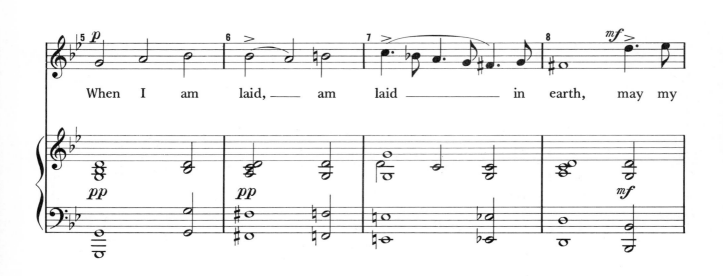

When I am laid, — am laid ——— in earth, may my

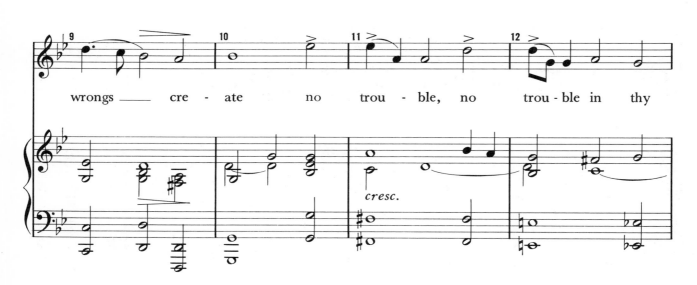

wrongs —— cre - ate no trou - ble, no trou - ble in thy

ah! ___ for ___ get ___ my fate. Re - mem - ber me, but

ah! _____ for - get my ___ fate.

* Low voices sing small notes.

O MISTRESS MINE

William Shakespeare

Roger Quilter
(1877—1953)

PASSING BY

Robert Herrick

Edward Purcell
(1689–1740)

Andante con moto

1. There is a la - dy
2. Her ges-tures, mo - tions,

sweet and kind, was nev - er face so pleased my mind; I
and her smiles, Her wit, her voice my heart __ be - guiles, Be -

did __ but see her pass - ing by, And yet I love her
guiles __ my heart, I know not why,

209

To Armando Rivas

LITTLE LAMB

William Blake

Wallace De Pue

Lit-tle lamb who made thee? Dost thou know who made thee?

Dost thou know who made thee? Gave thee life and

bid thee feed by the stream and o'er the mead Gave thee cloth-ing

THE VAGABOND

Robert Louis Stevenson

Ralph Vaughan Williams
(1872—1958)

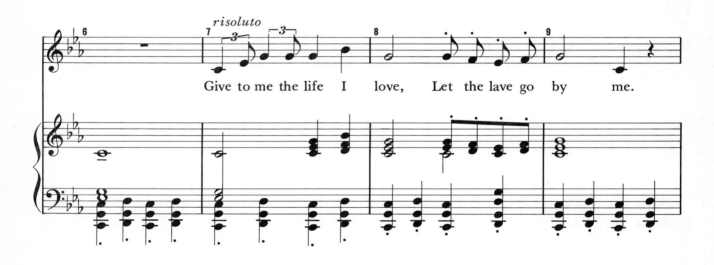

Give to me the life I love, Let the lave go by me.

Give the jol - ly heaven a - bove, And the by - way nigh me.

Bed in the bush with stars to see, Bread I dip in the ri - ver, There's the life for a man like me, There's the life for ev - er.

Let the blow fall soon or late, Let what will be o'er me;

Give the face of earth a - round, And the road be - fore me.

Wealth I seek not, hope nor love, Nor a ___ friend to know

me; All I seek, the heaven a - bove, ___ And the

road be - low me Or let

hope nor love, Nor a friend to know me; All I ask, the heaven a - bove, And the road be - low me.

O LORD MOST HOLY
Panis Angelicus

César Franck
(1822—1890)

O Lord most ho - ly,
Pa - nis an - ge - li - cus

To Wallace, Jr.

LULLABY

Wallace De Pue

Sleep now, lit - tle ba - by, close your sleep - y eyes. Sand - man's wait - ing for you with a big sur - prise. He'll take you to dream - land

fly - ing through the night_____ to find, Hid-den in slum - ber,

vi - sions of___ de - light.   Ice - cream moun-tains and so - da foun-tains and

can - dy or-chards you'll see   Choc-o-late makers and   ap-ple pie bak-ers are

a little faster

faster

SILENT NOON

Dante Gabriel Rossetti

Ralph Vaughan Williams

peace. The pas-ture gleams and glooms 'Neath bil - low-ing

skies that scat - ter and a - mass.

Poco più mosso

All round our nest, far as the eye can pass, Are

Quasi Recitative

Deep in the sun-searched growths the drag-on-fly ___ Hangs ___ like a blue thread loos-ened from the sky: ___ So ___ this winged hour is dropt to us from a-bove. ___

DOWN AMONG THE DEAD MEN

Anonymous

Traditional English "Drinking Song"

1. Here's a health to the Queen and a last-ing peace, To fac-tion an end, to wealth in-crease; Come, let's drink it while we've breath, For there's no drink-ing

2. Let charm-ing beau-ty's health go round, In whom Ce-les-tial joys are found; And may con-fu-sion still pur-sue The sense-less wo-man-

3. In smil-ing Bac-chus' joys I'll roll, De-ny no plea-sure to my soul; Let Bac-chus' health round swift-ly move, For Bac-chus is a

231

SEA - SHELL

Amy Lowell

Carl Engel
(1883—1944)

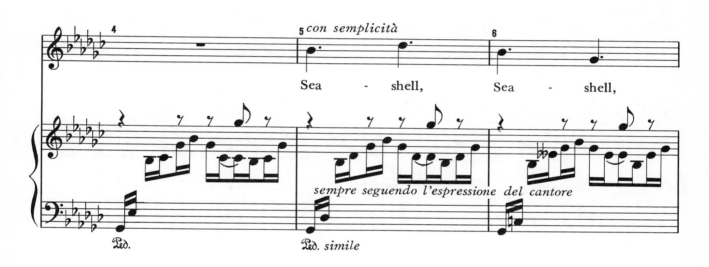

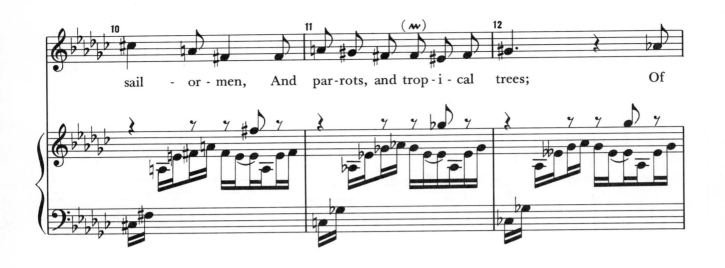

sail - or - men, And par-rots, and trop - i - cal trees; Of

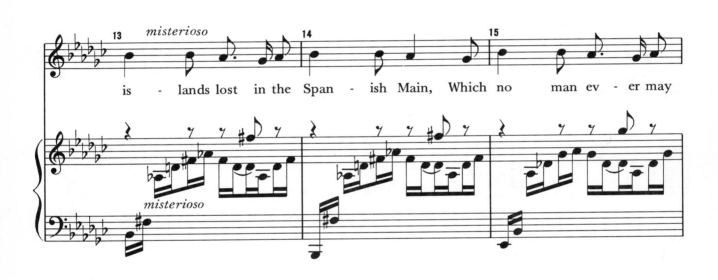

is - lands lost in the Span - ish Main, Which no man ev - er may

find a - gain, Of fish - es and cor - als un - der the waves, And

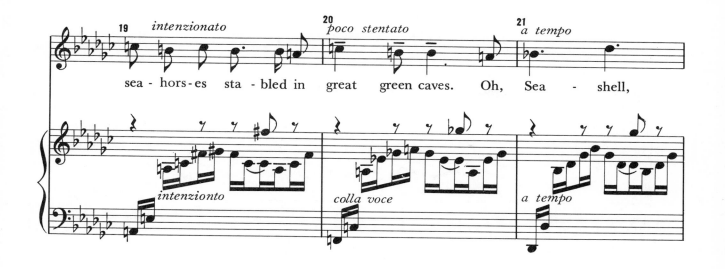

sea - hors - es sta - bled in great green caves. Oh, Sea - shell,

Sea - shell, Sing of the things you know _____ so

well. _____

THE HOUR OF DREAMING
L'Heure exquise

Reynaldo Hahn
(1875—1947)

show, Where winds are weep - ing: Oh love!_____ art
noir Où le vent pleu - re..... Rê - vons!_____ c'est

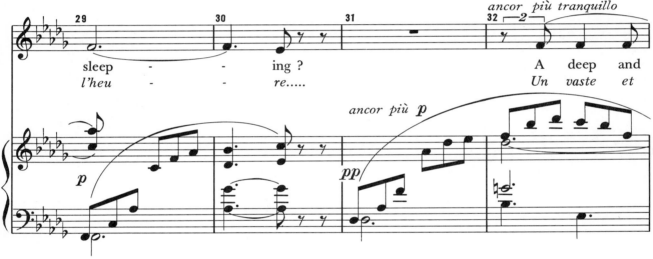

sleep - - ing? A deep and
l'heu - - re..... Un vaste et

ten - der Calm now lies O'er___ all things un - der Yon arch - ing
ten - dre A-pai-se - ment Sem - ble des - cen - dre Du fir - ma -

skies Where stars are gleam - ing:
ment Que l'astre i - ri - se.....

Oh hour of dream - - - ing!
C'est l'heu - re ex - qui - - - se.

239

THE SLEEP THAT FLITS ON BABY'S EYES

Rabindranath Tagore

John Alden Carpenter
(1876–1951)

Ancora più mosso ♩ = 112

Yes, there is a ru-mour that it has its dwell-ing where, in the fair-y vil-lage a-mong the shad-ows of the for-est dim-ly lit with glow-worms,

il basso sempre **p**

rall.

ELDORADO

Edgar Allan Poe

Wallace De Pue

met a pil - grim shad - ow. ____ "Shad-ow," said he, "Where can it be This

Land _____ of El - do - ra-do?" ____

"O - ver the moun - tains Of the Moon,

Down the Val - ley of the Shad - ow, Ride, bold-ly ride," The

shade re-plied, "If you seek for El - do - ra-do!"___

SELECTED, GRADED, AND CATEGORIZED LIST OF SONGS

Grades: A—advanced
B—medium
C—fairly easy

Grade is an attempt to indicate technical difficulty only and is at best a nebulous procedure. It is not intended as an index of musical and dramatic insight required for each song. It should be viewed only as a general guide for technical difficulty. Collections are not graded. A key to publishers is at the end of the list. Certain songs in each category may be sung by other voices.

Soprano Solo (Specify *high* key when ordering.)

Grade A

Composer	Title	Publisher
Bach, J. S.	*My Heart Ever Faithful*	GS
Bach-LaForge	*Now the Sheep Secure Are Grazing*	CF
Beergsma	*Doll's Boys Asleep*	CF
Debussy	*Beau Soir*	GS
Delibes	*Les Filles de Cadiz*	GS
Dello Joio	*All Things Leave Me*	CF
Duke	*The Mountains Are Dancing*	CF
Gluck	*O del mio dolce ardor*	GS
Handel	*Care Selve*	CF
Handel	*Come Unto Me*	GS
Handel	*I Know That My Redeemer Liveth*	GS
Handel	*Rejoice Greatly*	GS
Handel	*Sempre dolce ed amarose*	GS
Haydn	*With Verdure Clad*	GS
Head, M.	*The Piper*	BH
Head, M.	*The Singer*	BH
Mendelssohn	*Hear Ye Israel*	GS
Mozart	*Alleluia*	GS
Puccini	*O My Beloved Daddy*	Bel
Puccini	*One Fine Day*	GS
Puccini	*Musetta's Waltz*	Bel
Strauss	*All Soul's Day*	TP
Verdi	*Caro Nome*	GS

Grade B

Composer	Title	Publisher
Barber, S.	*Sure on This Shining Night*	GS
Bishop	*Lo, Hear the Gentle Lark*	GS
Brahms	*A Thought Like Music*	TP
Campbell-Tipton	*Spirit Flower*	GS
Charles	*Let My Song Fill Your Heart*	GS
Delibes	*Bonjour, Suzon*	CF
Diamond, D.	*Brigid's Song*	Mer
Elwell, H.	*All Foxes*	GS
Elwell, H.	*The Glittering Grief*	GS
Elwell, H.	*Phoenix Afire*	GS
Gounod	*O Divine Redeemer*	CF
Handel	*Come and Trip It*	BH
Handel	*Oh, Had I Jubal's Lyre*	GS
Handel	*Angels Ever Bright and Fair*	GS

Composer	Title	Publisher
Handel	*Verdant Meadows*	W-7
Haydn	*She Never Told Her Love*	GS
Malotte	*The Beatitudes*	GS
Malotte	*The Twenty-third Psalm*	GS
Monroe	*Hopak*	GS
Mozart	*From Out of Thy Casement Glancing*	GS
Purcell	*Man Is From Woman Made*	BH
Rachmaninoff	*Lilacs*	GS
Schubert	*Hark, Hark the Lark*	TP
Strauss, R.	*Devotion*	TP
Strauss, R.	*Tomorrow*	TP
Wolf	*Verborgenheit*	TP
Yon	*O Faithful Cross*	JF

Grade C

Composer	Title	Publisher
Bach-Prout	*In Faith I Quiet Wait*	Gal
Barber, S.	*The Daisies*	GS
Beethoven	*I Love Thee*	GS
Brahms	*Lullaby*	TP
Brahms	*Sandmannchen*	GS
Dawson (arr.)	*Jesus Walked This Lonesome Valley*	W-7
Dungan	*Where Is My Heart?*	Bel
Grieg	*Ein Schwann*	CF
Head, M.	*A Slumber Song of the Madonna*	BH
Humperdinck	*Evening Prayer*	CF
MacDowell	*Thy Beaming Eyes*	CF
Mozart	*Cradle Song*	GS
Purcell	*Nymphs and Shepherds*	Ox
Schubert	*Thou Art Repose*	GS
Thompson, R.	*My Master Hath a Garden*	ECS
Thompson, R.	*Velvet Shoes*	ECS
Thiman	*Thou Wilt Keep Him in Perfect Peace*	HWG

Mezzo-Soprano Solo (Specify *medium* key when ordering.)

Composer	Title	Publisher
Bach-Kramer	*Sheep May Safely Graze*	Gal
Bach-Lebell	*The Heart That Thou Hast Given*	Gal
Bantock	*A Feast of Lanterns*	Gal
Bowling	*He Shall Be Like a Tree*	CF
Carpenter	*When I Bring to You Colored Toys*	GS
Charles	*Over the Land Is April*	Wil
Dvořák	*I Will Sing New Songs of Gladness*	AMP
Gaul	*Eye Hath Not Seen*	GS
Gluck	*Che Faro sen*	GS
Guion	*At the Cry of the First Bird*	GS
Hageman	*At the Well*	GS
Handel	*Care Selve*	CF
Handel	*Lord, to Thee Each Night and Day*	Gal
Mendelssohn	*O for the Wings of a Dove*	GS
Moore	*Old Song*	CF
Mozart	*Voi Che Sapete*	GS
Olmstead	*Thy Sweet Singing*	GS
Pergolesi	*Se Tu M'ami*	GS
Schubert	*Serenade*	GS
Schubert	*To Music*	Ox

Composer	Title	Publisher
Spross	*Let All My Life Be Music*	TP
Thomas	*Knowest Thou Not That Fair Land?*	GS
Thomas	*My True Love Hath My Heart*	BH
Ware	*This Day Is Mine*	Bos
Watts	*The Little Shepherd's Song*	Bel
Whelpley	*The Nightingale Has a Lyre of Gold*	Bos

Grade B

Composer	Title	Publisher
Bantock	*Silent Strings*	BH
Charles	*Let My Song Fill Your Heart*	GS
Crist	*April Rain*	CF
Curran	*Gratitude*	GS
Davis, K.K.	*I Have a Fawn*	Gal
Delibes	*Passepied*	GS
Dvořák	*Lord, Thou Art My Refuge* (Biblical Songs)	AMP
Edmonds	*I Know My Love*	CF
German, E.	*Who'll Buy My Lavender*	Wil
Gibbs	*Evening in Summer*	Ox
Handel	*He Shall Feed His Flock*	GS
Haydn	*My Mother Bids Me Bind My Hair*	CF
Horn	*Cherry Ripe*	GS
Hunt	*Only the Children Know*	Bel
Liadoff	*Musical Snuff Box*	GS
Mendelssohn	*On Wings of Song*	GS
Niles	*Wayfaring Stranger*	GS
Quilter	*Music When Soft Voices Die*	BH
Scott	*Lullaby*	Gal
Thiman	*The God of Love My Shepherd Is*	HWG
Van de Water	*The Publican*	TP
Weaver	*Moon-Marketing*	GS

Grade C

Composer	Title	Publisher
Barber	*The Daisies*	GS
Boyce-Taylor	*What Beauties Doth My Nymph Disclose*	Ox
Chanler	*The Lamb*	AMP
Coates	*Bird Songs at Eventide*	Chp
Copland	*Simple Gifts*	BH
Dolmetsch	*Have You Seen But a White Lily Grow*	GS
Edmonds	*Fare You Well*	CF
Fauré	*Adieu*	GS
Codard	*Florian's Song*	GS
Haydn	*She Never Told Her Love*	GS
MacGimsey	*Sweet Little Jesus Boy* (V. 1234)	CF
Peterkin	*I Heard a Piper Piping*	Ox
Pinkham, D.	*Elegy*	ECS
Raynor	*An Old Lullaby*	Ox
Scott	*Think on Me*	Wil
Shaw, C.	*Since First I Saw Your Face*	CF
Speaks	*Morning*	GS
Taylor, D.	*La Petite Robe*	JF
Thompson, R.	*My Master Hath a Garden*	ECS
Thompson, R.	*Velvet Shoes*	ECS
Thomson, V.	*My Shepherd Will Supply My Need*	HWG
Van de Water	*The Penitent*	TP
Vaughan Williams	*Linden Lea*	BH

Alto Solo (Specify *low* key when ordering.)

Grade A

Composer	Title	Publisher
Agay, D.	*The Yankee Peddlar*	MS
Bach-Kramer	*Sheep May Safely Graze*	Gal
Bantock	*A Feast of Lanterns*	Gal
Bantock	*Silent Strings*	BH
Barber	*I Hear an Army*	GS
Berger	*Heart*	Brd
Berger	*Lonely People*	Brd
Bizet	*Habañera*	GS
Bridge	*Go Not Happy Day*	Bos
Bridge	*Love Went A-Riding*	BH
Davis, K.	*The Deaf Old Woman*	Gal
Dougherty	*Loveliest of Trees*	BH
Dunn	*The Bitterness of Love*	JF
Dvořák	*God Is My Shepherd* (Biblical Songs)	GS
Dvořák	*Hear My Prayer, O Lord* (Biblical Songs)	GS
Gluck	*O Del Mio Dolce Ardor*	GS
Grieg	*With a Water Lily*	GS
Hageman	*Miranda*	Gal
Kramer	*Swans*	Bel
Loughborough	*How Lovely Is the Hand of God*	TP
Purcell	*I Attempt from Love's Sickness to Fly*	GS
Schumann	*The Lotus Flower*	GS
Scott	*Lullaby*	Gal
Strauss, R.	*Serenade*	GS
Thomas	*Connais-tu le pays?*	GS

Grade B

Composer	Title	Publisher
Dunhill	*The Cloths of Heaven*	Gal
Elgar	*Where Corals Lie*	Nov
Gretchaninoff	*Slumber Song*	CF
Harty	*My Pagan Love*	BH
Horn	*I've Been Roaming*	TP
Ives	*Night Song*	SMC
Morgan	*Clorinda*	BH
Naginski	*The Pasture*	GS
Owens	*Laudamus*	Bos
Ronald	*O Lovely Night*	BH
Schubert	*An Die Musik* (in collection)	BH
Sjoberg	*Visions*	Gal
Tosti	*The Last Song*	Bel
Tyson	*Sea Moods*	GS
Whelpley	*The Nightingale Has a Lyre of Gold*	Bos

Grade C

Composer	Title	Publisher
Barber	*The Daisies*	GS
Bernstein, L.	*It Must Be Me*	GS
Charles	*Sweet Song of Long Ago*	GS
Dodge, M. & J.	*Gossiping*	Wil
Dougherty	*The Minor Bird*	GS
Ferrari	*The Mirror*	Mks
Gibbs	*Give Eyes*	Bos

Composer	Title	Publisher
Martin	*Crown of the Year*	BH
Niles	*Go 'Way from My Window*	GS
Quilter	*Fuchsia Tree*	BH
Stanford	*Soft Day*	Gal
Thiman	*God of Love My Shepherd Is*	HWG
Weill	*The Lonesome Dove*	GS
Vaughan Williams	*Linden Lea*	BH

Tenor Solo (Specify *high* key when ordering.)

Grade A

Barber	*Sure on This Shining Night*	GS
Bassett	*Take Joy Home*	GS
Brahms	*The May Night*	GS
Bridge	*Love Went A-Riding*	BH
Charles	*My Lady Walks in Loveliness*	GS
Grieg	*A Swan*	GS
Guion	*At the Cry of the First Bird*	GS
Guion	*I Talked to God Last Night*	GS
Hageman	*Christ Went Up into the Hills*	CF
Harker	*How Beautiful upon the Mountains*	GS
Ireland	*Sea Fever*	Gal
Laddle	*How Lovely Are Thy Dwellings*	BH
Mendelssohn	*If With All Your Hearts*	GS
Menotti	*The Hero*	GS
Noble	*Grieve Not the Holy Spirit*	HWG
O'Hara	*Bright Is the Ring of Words*	CF
Pergolesi	*Nina*	GS
Quilter	*Fear No More the Sun*	BH
Quilter	*Go Lovely Rose*	Chp
Rachmaninoff	*In the Silence of the Night*	GS
Rogers	*Great Peace Have They*	GS
Sacco	*Brother Will, Brother John*	GS
Schubert	*Serenade*	GS
Walton	*Under the Greenwood Tree*	BH
Wood	*A Bird Sang in the Rain*	Chp
Young-Wilson	*Phyllis Has Such a Charming Grace*	BH

Grade B

Bach-LaForge	*Now the Sheep Secure Are Grazing*	CF
Ball	*Who Knows*	W-7
Bantock	*Silent Strings*	BH
Bitgood	*Give Me Faith*	HWG
Britten	*The Ash Grove*	BH
Britten	*The Plough Boy*	BH
Chadwick	*A Ballad of Trees and the Master*	TP
Coates	*Bird Song at Eventide*	Chp
Coates	*I Hear You Singing*	Chp
Cox	*To a Hilltop*	GS
Elliot	*Spring's a Lovable Lady*	W-7
Forsyth	*The Bellman*	TP
Hahn	*Were My Songs with Wings Provided*	GS
Hamblen	*This Is My Commandment*	CF
Handel	*Silent Worship*	JF

Composer	Title	Publisher
Head	*When I Think upon the Maidens*	BH
Keel	*Trade Winds*	BH
Klemm	*A Hundred Little Loves*	CF
McFayden	*Home*	SHM
Malotte	*The Twenty-Third Psalm*	GS
Matthews	*The Lord Is My Shepherd*	SF
Schubert	*Serenade*	GS
Secchi	*Love Me or Not*	BH
Sinding	*Sylvelin*	TP
Spross	*Let All My Life Be Music*	TP

Grade C

Composer	Title	Publisher
Barber	*The Daisies*	GS
Bury	*There Is a Lady*	CF
Darm	*Whenever My Mary Goes By*	BH
Densmore	*Roadways*	TP
Diack	*All in the April Evening*	BH
Dickson	*Thanks Be To God*	BH
Dougherty	*Rio Grande*	GS
Edwards	*Dedication*	GS
Handel	*When First We Met*	Ox
Haydn	*To Friendship*	W-7
Hormer	*Sheep and Lambs*	GS
Legrenzi	*Che Feiro Costume*	TP
Liddle	*An Old French Carol*	BH
Lully	*Sombre Woods*	GS
Martini	*The Joys of Love*	GS
Mendelssohn	*On Wings of Song*	CF
Morgan	*Clorinda*	BH
Niles	*The Black Oak Tree*	CF
Quilter	*The Ash Grove*	BH
Tosti	*Serenade*	GS
Willan	*O Perfect Love*	HWG
Wilson	*Mary of Allendale*	BH

Baritone Solo (Specify *medium* key when ordering.)

Grade A

Composer	Title	Publisher
Barab	*A Main Me Loved*	BH
Britten	*The Plough Boy*	BH
Britten	*The Ship of Rio*	Ox
Charles	*Incline Thine Ear*	GS
Dougherty	*Shenandoah*	GS
Dvořák	*Turn Thee to Me* (Biblical Songs)	AMP
Gore	*Entreat Me Not To Leave Thee*	Con
Handel	*Silent Worship*	GS
Haydn	*Now Heaven in Fullest Glory*	GS
Landon	*O Lovely Night*	BH
Malotte	*Song of the Open Road*	Brn
Niles	*Gambler, Don't Lose Your Place*	GS
Niles	*The Rovin' Gambler*	GS
Purcell	*An Evening Hymn*	HWG
Quilter	*Blow, Blow Thou Winter Wind* (Shakespeare Songs)	BH
Quilter	*Come Away Death* (Shakespeare Songs)	BH

Composer	Title	Publisher
Schumann	*Two Grenadiers*	GS
Schumann	*Widmung*	GS
Scott	*Come Ye Blessed*	GS
Scott	*The Old Road*	GS
Strauss, R.	*Morgen*	GS
Tyson	*Sea Moods*	GS
Vaughan Williams	*The Roadside Fire*	BH
Warlock	*My Own Country*	Ox

Grade B

Composer	Title	Publisher
Beethoven	*In Questa Tomba*	GS
Bridge	*O That It Were So*	Chp
Dougherty	*Blow Ye Winds*	GS
Dougherty	*Mobile Bay*	GS
Dvořák	*I Will Sing New Songs of Gladness* (Biblical Songs)	AMP
Dvořák	*Sing Ye a Joyful Song* (Biblical Songs)	AMP
Edmunds	*Praise We the Lord*	CF
Head	*Acquaint Now Thyself with Him*	BH
Head	*Money*	BH
Head	*Thus Spake Jesus*	BH
Hely-Hutchinson	*Old Mother Hubbard*	CF
Homer	*Banjo Song*	GS
Keel	*Trade Winds*	BH
Leoni	*Tally Ho*	GS
Martini	*Plaisir D'Amour*	GS
Morgan	*Clorinda*	BH
Scott	*Lullaby*	Gal
Thiman	*The God of Love My Shepherd Is*	HWG
Thiman	*Jesus the Very Thought of Thee*	HWG
Vaughan Williams	*Whither Must I Wander*	GS

Grade C

Composer	Title	Publisher
American Folk	*Jesus, Jesus Rest Your Head*	CF
Clarke	*The Blind Ploughman*	Chp
Dix	*The Trumpeter*	CF
Dougherty	*Across the Western Ocean*	GS
Dougherty	*Colorado Trail*	GS
Dvořák	*Hear My Prayer* (Biblical Songs)	AMP
Forsythe	*Tell Me Not a Lovely Lass*	HWG
German	*Rolling Down to Rio*	CF
Handel	*Verdant Meadows*	W-7
Niles	*The Gamblers' Lament*	GS
Porter	*Music When Soft Voiles Die*	TP
Purcell	*Next Winter Comes Slowly*	Int
Taylor	*May Day Carol*	JF
Vaughan Williams	*Linden Lea*	BH

Bass Solo (Specify *low* key when ordering.)

Grade A

Composer	Title	Publisher
Brahms	*O Tod Vie Bitter* (Four Serious Songs)	GS
Debussy	*Beau Soir*	Bos
Fauré	*The Cradles*	W-7
Lully	*Bois Epais*	BH

Composer	Title	Publisher
Schubert	*Whither*	GS
Sowerby	*The Lord Is My Shepherd* (Three Songs For Bass)	HWG
Strauss, R.	*Zueignung*	GS
Tschaikowsky	*Pilgrim Song*	GS
Wolfe	*De Glory Road*	GS

Grade B

Banks	*A Prayer for St. Francis*	HWG
Carpenter	*May the Maiden*	TP
Chales	*The Sussex Sailor*	GS
Clarke	*The Blind Ploughman*	Chp
Dvořàk	*Hear My Prayer* (Biblical Songs)	AMP
Head	*Sweet Chance that Led My Steps*	BH
Lehman	*Myself When Young*	Bos
MacDermid	*In My Father's House Are Many Mansions*	For
McGill	*Duna*	BH
Thiman	*Thou Wilt Keep Him in Perfect Peace*	HWG
Ware	*This Day Is Mine*	Bos
Vaughan Williams	*The Roadside Fire*	BH

Grade C

Bach	*Come Sweet Death*	CF
Britten	*The Sally Gardens*	BH
Brown	*Twenty-Third Psalm*	HWG
Dodson	*Across the Western Ocean*	GS
Dougherty	*Blow Ye Winds*	GS
Dougherty	*Three Candles*	Bos
Hall	*Go to the Well*	Bos
Keel	*Trade Winds*	BH
Pergolesi	*Nina*	TP
Thiman	*The God of Love My Shepherd Is*	HWG
Wellesley	*Sing Me a Chantey*	SF

COLLECTIONS

Title	Publisher
Album of Sacred Songs, Vol. 1384, High; Vol. 1385, Low	GS
Anthology of Italian Song, Books I and II	GS
Anthology of Modern French Songs (ed. Spicker), Vol. I, High; Vol. II, Low	GS
Art Songs for School and Studio (Glenn and Sprouse), First Year, High and Low; Second Year, High and Low	TP
Bass Songs (ed. Mason)	TP
Brahms: Fifty Selected Songs, Vol. 1581, Low; Vol. 1582, High	GS
Fifty Art Songs	GS
Fifty-Five Art Songs (Spaeth and Thompson)	SB
Fifty-Six Songs You Like To Sing	GS
Folk Songs of the British Isles	BH
Foster, Stephen: Album of Songs, Twenty Favorites	GS
Franz, Robert: Vocal Album, Vol. 1572, High; Vol. 1573, Low	GS
French Art Songs for School and Studio (ed. Glenn and Taylor)	TP
Music for Sight Singing (Ottman)	P-H

Title	Publisher
Operatic Anthology (ed. Spicker), Vol. I, Soprano; Vol. II, Mezzo Soprano or Alto; Vol. III, Tenor; Vol. IV, Baritone; Vol. V Bass	GS
Pathways of Song (LaForge and Earhart), Vol. I–IV, each for High and Low	W-7
Schubert, Franz: Twenty-Four Favorite Songs, Vol. 350 High; Vol. 351 Low	GS
Sight Reading, See and Sing, Vols. I–III (Ehret)	Pro
Solo Singer, The (Wilson), Vols. I and II, High and Low	CF
Standard Vocal Repetoire	W-7
Twentieth Century Art Songs	GS
Useful Teaching Songs (Lehmann), Vol. I, Soprano; Vol. II, Mezzo Soprano; Vol. III, Alto; Vol. IV, Tenor; Vol. V, Bass	Chp
Young Singer, The (R 8062)	CF

KEY TO PUBLISHERS

AMP	Associated Music Publishers, Inc.
BH	Boosey & Hawkes, Inc.
Bel	Belwin, Inc.
Bos	Boston Music Co.
Brd	Broude Bos.
Brn	Bourne, Inc.
CF	Carl Fischer, Inc.
Chp	Chappell and Co., Inc.
Con	Concordia Publishing House
ECS	E. C. Schirmer Music Co.
For	Forrester Music Corp.
GS	G. Schirmer, Inc.
Gal	Galaxy Music Corp.
HWG	H. W. Gray Co., Inc.
Int	International Music Corp.
JF	J. Fischer & Bros.
MS	Music Sales, Inc.
Mer	Mercury Music Corp.
Mks	Edward B. Marks Music Corp.
Nov	Novello (order from HWG)
Ox	Oxford University Press
P-H	Prentice-Hall, Inc.
Pro	Pro-Art Publications
SB	Summy-Birchard Publishing Co.
SF	Sam Fox Publishing Co.
SHM	Schmitt, Hall & McCreary Co.
SMC	Southern Music Co. of New York
TP	Theodore Presser Co.
W-7	Warner Bros. 7 Arts Music
Wil	Willis Music Co.